Principle-Based Refactoring

Learning Software Design Principles by Applying Refactoring Rules

Steve Halladay

Principle Publishing
Park City, Utah

The author and publisher have taken care in preparing this book, however they make no expressed or implied warranty of any kind and assume no responsibility for errors or omissions. No liability is assumed for incidental or consequential damages in connection with or arising from the use of the information or programs contained herein.

ISBN-10 061569022X
ISBN-13 978-0615690223
4th Printing December 2013

To those who seek
to go beyond hacking
into the realm of pure thought…

Contents

—

List of Rules

Preface

Several years ago I helped teach an introductory programming course. This was my first experience teaching introductory students and I found it fascinating. Part of the class was project-based and I convinced the other faculty members to use a chess game as the target for the project. I suggested chess because of its opportunity to illustrate many Object Oriented concepts.

I correctly assumed that a chess program would be a challenging project for introductory programming students. But what I did not anticipate was the types of programming constructs I would see coming out of these introductory students. I had been in the software development industry for decades and had had very little dealing with novice programmers. Many of the concepts that had become second nature to me were very foreign to these students.

Because these concepts were second nature to me, I found it very difficult to articulate them. As I reviewed students' code, I found myself at a loss to be able to explain to the students why they should not do what they were doing. Sometimes all I could really tell a student was "don't do that". The students would respond, "then what should I do?" I was able to show the students what to do instead, but I still found it difficult to explain why.

As I worked with more of these students I noticed various patterns emerging in their code. I started to make a list of the issues as well as what to do instead. What emerged was the fundamental notion of a rule: when X happens, do Y.

I found I had to be very careful with these rules because students would observe them very literally. For example, when I would try to help students understand the notions of abstraction I would tell them to keep their methods to seven lines instead of fifty line monstrosities. I soon found students that would still write the long methods and then arbitrarily divide them into seven line chunks named method1, method2, etc. They were indeed following the rule, but had entirely missed the point.

About this time I became acquainted with Martin Fowler's book entitled *Refactoring, Improving the Design of Existing Code*. While I found this book to be extremely helpful (clearly a motivation for this work and I have used many of the rules he identifies herein), I found that some of the rules in the book contradict each other – at least in the literal sense. I could imagine the same students who followed my rules so literally having a difficult time resolving these seeming inconsistencies.

Further I found that I disagreed with Fowler on some counts. Some of the rules I felt would be detrimental to my students. As I worked more with faculty and students I found that I disagreed with them from time to time on various rules as well. In fact, our differences became a bit of a joke as we traded jabs back and forth, talking trash about the others' perspectives. Still, I was troubled. Which rules *should* apply?

I felt I had a duty to my students to try figure out a basis for deciding which rules to apply. I thought long and hard about the rules and as I did so, I started to realize similarities between them. For example, I noticed that normalizing a database somehow felt like extracting a reusable or redundant code segment. This realization led me to try and clump these rules together in ways that somehow felt right.

Once I had clumps of related rules, I tried to identify what made the rules belong to the same clump. Eventually I was able to articulate a notion – what I am calling a principle, which seemed to support the rules. Having identified the principle, I was then able to take another look at the rules and more clearly categorize them. The result is what I present in this text.

As I have pondered rules, how they behave and interrelate, I have come to realize that the rules merely outline principles. During my career in the software development industry I had developed an understanding of the principles that manifested themselves as intuition. It wasn't until I started teaching that I tried to reduce the intuition to a set of rules. The reason I used rules instead of intuition was that I could not directly articulate the intuition, but I could explain the rules so that they would give an outline of my intuition.

Each rule in this book has three sections. The first section is an abstract, which is a brief summary of the essence of the rule. The intent is that the reader may use this section as a reference to recall the gist of the rule.

The next section describing each rule is a discussion of the rule. This section explains how to think about the rule as well as some of its implications.

The third section of the rule is an example to illustrate the rule. The example is not meant to be completely concrete. In fact, the example code will not execute since it omits many of the syntactical details of an actual programming language. This is intentional. The idea is to focus on the important aspects of the rules without worrying about programming language details.

The other chapters of the book give a few other ideas and insights that may be helpful. Chapter one tries to illustrate the need for principles. Chapter two introduces the principles. Chapter three talks about mechanics of refactoring and gives some helpful guidelines for unit testing. Chapters four through eleven explain the refactoring rules organized by the main principle influencing each rule. Notice that many principles may influence a specific rule. The organization of the rules into principle-based chapters is an attempt to find the main principle for each rule, but should not be viewed as absolutely the only influence. Chapter twelve reiterates the importance of principles over rules. Appendix A is a brief discussion of a software design pyramid that may serve students of software design by helping them identify their progression and maturation.

Computer Science is about conceptualizing systems and being able to communicate those conceptualizations. Hopefully, the rules and principles in this text will contribute to helping us all better conceptualize systems and communicate about our conceptualizations.

Chapter 1 - Introduction

Imagine a couple of programmers, Fred and Wilma, who are pair-programming. They have been working on their company's latest mobile app; a program that delivers customer specific, data-mined information from the company's main server. Since their company could not really define the requirements clearly, the company wanted an app they could show customers so as to get feedback from them. Fred and Wilma have built three versions of the app iteratively, and they have refined the app with each iteration.

While this iterative development approach has been great for determining customer requirements, it has prevented Fred and Wilma from creating a comprehensive design from the start. So now the code they have been developing has been stretched and contorted in ways they had not anticipated. It is difficult for the developers to make more modifications; the class structure is convoluted and the methods no longer have simple specific functions. It is time for them to refactor.

As they sit in front of a computer with Fred at the keyboard, Wilma suggests adding a parameter to a function to make it clearer what the function is doing. Fred is resistant to this suggestion because the parameter Wilma wants to add already is a private field within the class. Wilma would like to remove the field and pass the value as a parameter, but Fred reasons that it is easier to just leave the value as a field. Let's eaves drop on their conversation.

"Fred," Wilma says, "I think making the field a parameter makes it clearer what the function is doing."

"How so?" Fred asks.

Wilma responds, "The parameter makes it clear what the inputs to the method are. If we leave the value as a field, the method can still use the value, but it's sort of hidden."

"Yeah," Fred says, "but isn't it more Object-Oriented to use a field instead of a parameter? Parameters feel so... procedural."

Wilma asks, "What do you mean by 'more Object-Oriented'? I don't even know what that means. I program in Java and C#, so I know what Object-Oriented Programming is, but how can code be more or less Object-Oriented?"

"I don't know," Fred says, "but I was reading on reallyObjectOrientedProgrammingStuff.com and they said we should be more Object-Oriented. So I decided my style is going to be more OO."

"So," Wilma asks, "Does being more OO mean we shouldn't use parameters for methods? Should we only use fields?"

"Well," Fred responds, "Probably not for everything. We should use parameters where they make sense. In this case, it makes more sense to use a field since we already have a field. See, it's more OO."

"I don't get it," Wilma says, "My style may not be as OO as yours, but I think it makes more sense to show exactly what a method needs to be able to perform its task."

Fred says, "I guess it's really just a question of style and what works for you. You have your style and I have mine. I guess neither one is better or worse – just different."

"That may be," Wilma responds, "But how is a person supposed to figure out what style makes sense. How can it really just be what makes sense to you or to me? Isn't one approach really better than the other? Isn't there some

2

guiding principle that can help us to determine how to build the best software?"

Wilma's final question drives to the heart of the problem. Is software development really a stylistic and personal preference-based activity, or are there actual engineering principles that distinguish better software?

In 1999, Martin Fowler published a book entitled *Refactoring, Improving the Design of Existing Code*. This book does a great job of introducing refactoring and gives 72 rules for refactoring. I have used this text extensively in my software design classes to motivate understanding software design; rather than teach design from the top-down as an academic exercise, I have found it helpful to start with existing code and back into software design principles.

As I have used Fowler's text in my design classes, I have often heard conversations very similar to that of Fred and Wilma above. In these conversations, students come to an impasse and decide to agree to disagree while chalking it up to personal preference.

These conversations are not unique to students. I have frequently heard and participated in these conversations over a career lasting decades. And even though I have experienced these same conversations, I can't help but realize that software design is not merely personal preference. Some software really does seem to be better than other – it's not just a tomāto/tomăto situation.

By rejecting the notion of personal preference as a basis for software design, we are left to cast about and determine concrete criteria for what we do to and with our software designs. We need to find solid principles for our decisions that always lead to arguably better designs. This book attempts to do just that.

One of the problems with explaining principles lies in their ethereal nature. Principles give a general direction or a general flavor, but avoid delineation. Trying to concretely define a principle is like trying to determine the precise edge of a cloud. On the other hand, rules are very concrete. A rule usually has the form "if you are in this situation, you should do this".

The relationship between rules and principles is similar to lines that outline a drawing of an object. The lines are not the object and the object is not the lines, but the lines suggest the object; the lines help to define the object. So, if we want to understand a principle, it is helpful to enumerate rules that outline the principle.

We see the relationship between rules and principles as we consider the work of a novice versus that of an expert. A novice completes a task by following rules. Each time the state of the system in which the novice operates changes, the novice consults the rulebook and behaves accordingly. This works reasonably well, up to the point where the system enters a state that the rulebook does not describe. At this point the novice is at a loss for how to proceed.

On the other hand, the expert is not focused on rules because the expert is driven by principles. It's not that the expert purposely violates the rules. In fact, most of the time experts appear to follow the same rules as the novice, but from time to time observers of the expert will catch the expert violating a rule. The expert neither purposefully follows nor violates the rules - the expert is virtually oblivious to the rules.

The result of adhering to principles instead of following rules is that the expert can deal with previously unforeseen states. Instead of lacking a rule to define behavior for an unforeseen state, the expert uses the same principles in the novel state as the expert has used in any other state.

Over time, the reflective novice will extract and intuit the principles by following the rules. Since the rules outline the principle, as the novice begins to get a feel for the principle, the novice may interpolate between rules to formulate behavior for states not addressed by the concrete rules. However, once a novice develops enough intuition to make such interpolations, the novice is really no longer a pure novice, but is beginning to enter the realm of the expert.

This book attempts to teach principles both by direct discussion of the principle as well as by suggesting rules to outline the principles. The next chapter enumerates eight principles of software design. The following chapters identify rules for refactoring. These rules are based on and help to illuminate the principles.

Many of the rules in this book are adaptations from Fowler's work. This text eliminates some of Fowler's rules due to a lack of principle-based foundation. In addition to eliminating some rules, this text adds rules demanded by some of the principles.

The list of rules in this book is not exhaustive. In fact, that is the point of the book, not to have to enumerate all possible rules, but to enumerate enough rules to outline the principles. Once students of design understand the principles, they can forget the rules and adhere to the principles.

If this book is successful, the reader will begin to develop an intuition for the basic principles described in the next chapter. Then the reader will refine his or her intuition by considering the refactoring rules in the later chapters. As the reader's intuition develops, he or she will probably identify more rules that are helpful incarnations of the design principles. However, keep in mind that the ultimate goal is to abandon the rules and embrace the principles with confidence. Having mastered the design principles, the reader will become more effective not only in refactoring, but also in original software design.

Chapter 2 - Design Principles

If we were to study culinary arts, on the first day the instructor might start our curriculum by giving us a recipe and having us bake a cake. On the second day the instructor might give us a different recipe for an omelet. On the third day we might try a recipe for custard pie. At the end of these three days we might be asking ourselves, why is the instructor just giving us recipes? Couldn't we just look up these recipes online and cook anything we want?

On the fourth day we expect yet another recipe, but we are surprised. Instead of giving us another recipe, the instructor walks in and asks us what each of these recipes has in common. First, we might think about the kinds of food we have been cooking. Cakes and pies are desserts, but not omelets. We might consider the shape of the food. Cakes and pies are round, but omelets really are only round before they are folded. So what do these recipes have in common? As we examine the recipes again we realize that all three have eggs in common. Once we make this observation the instructor confirms our guess and asks what the effects of the eggs are in the recipes.

We think about the custard since it was the most recent experience and we notice how the eggs gave the custard stiffness. Then we think about the omelet and also notice how the eggs keep the ingredients together. In fact, now that we think about it, eggs also keep the cake ingredients together as well. So we suggest to the instructor that the effect of the eggs is to give the ingredients cohesiveness. The instructor gets a delighted look and exclaims that we are correct. The instructor tells us that we now understand egg-ness.

Over the next few days the instructor repeats the process for foods containing sweetness and then saltiness. Each time we come to appreciate the effects of some additive. However, once we realize there is cohesiveness, sweetness and saltiness, instead of introducing us to a fourth set of recipes, the instructor asks us about what each of the additives have in common.

This seems like a tricky question because each of the additives is different – that's what we had just learned. So how can all the additives have something in common? They each have a different effect on the food we are cooking – then it hits us. The thing that each ingredient has in common is that each has some specific effect on the resultant food. We point this out to the instructor and the instructor once again smiles and acknowledges our understanding by telling us that we now understand ingredient-ness.

The instructor goes on to explain that now that we understand that foods have different ingredients and each ingredient has a different effect, we no longer need only to follow recipes, but we can now also create new recipes!

This is how learning seems to work – we make observations and then generalize from specific observations to a more general concept. When we accumulate enough related general concepts we can then derive principles. Once we understand the principles we are prepared to apply the principles in novel ways.

Unlike the cooking instructor who started with specific recipes and moved to principles, this book will attempt to first introduce the principles followed by specific rules to outline the principles. This approach risks that the explanation of principles may be a bit confusing. However, the intent is to familiarize the reader with the principles *a priori* so as to expedite the formation of the principles while reviewing the refactoring rules. As you read through the explanation of the principles in this chapter, if principles are a little confusing it may be helpful to refer to the rules that are based on the principle.

You may also want to treat the principles' descriptions section of this chapter as a reference. As you read through the explanation of the rules in the later chapters, you may want to refer back to the principles it references. As you work back and forth, you will come to understand both the principles and their application.

Since this chapter serves as a reference, this chapter presents the principles in alphabetical order to make it easier to reference the principles.

Cohesion

Cohesion has to do with how focused a software module is. A module is a clump of software such as a block of code, a method, a class or even a package. Focus, in this instance, means how well does each subcomponent of the module relate to the overall purpose of the module. High cohesion indicates that all pieces of the module contribute to the overall purpose, while low cohesion indicates that few of the subcomponents of the module contribute to the module's purpose. High cohesion is desirable.

Larry Constantine first identified cohesion as a software design principle in 1975 as part of his structured design process. Constantine enumerated seven variations of cohesion ordered from low (less desirable) cohesion to high (more desirable) cohesion. These variants constitute a continuum and include:
- Coincidental cohesion
- Logical cohesion
- Temporal cohesion
- Procedural cohesion
- Communicational cohesion
- Sequential cohesion
- Functional cohesion

Coincidental Cohesion

Coincidental cohesion occurs when the subcomponents of a module have virtually nothing in common. As an illustration of coincidental cohesion, imagine a junk drawer in a kitchen. When you open the junk drawer, you might find a screwdriver, miscellaneous keys, a stick of chewing gum, a roll of packing tape, some sun block and a coupon for 50% off on a car wash. What do these items have in common? They have nothing in common except that they all reside in the junk drawer. The only reason these items are in the drawer is because the owner didn't know what else to do with them.

So it is with modules of coincidental cohesion. Examples of coincidental cohesion in code might include a "Main" class that contains the main method of a program as well as all other static methods the program may use. Inexperienced programmers often create these classes more by accident than on purpose. Programmers want to write a program and give little thought to the organization, so the coincidental cohesive module just sort of emerges from the lack of organized thinking.

Logical Cohesion

Modules with logical cohesion are those modules that have subcomponents that the developer grouped together because the subcomponents have the same categorization. For example, imagine a pantry with many shelves. Each shelf has a logical category of foods. On the top shelf are the drinks including soda pop, bottled water, energy drinks, fruit drinks and health drinks. On the next shelf are the ethnic foods. These include Mexican beans and peppers, Chinese sauces and Italian pasta and spices. The third shelf contains canned vegetables such as peas, carrots, olives and potatoes. Each of these three shelves is logically cohesive; the shelf contains items of the same category. So what is the problem with this organization? While there is nothing wrong with the organization, the shelf has little cohesion. For example, you usually will not use the Mexican foods in combination with the Chinese and Italian foods in a single meal, but you may use drinks from the top shelf, some ethnic foods from the second shelf and various vegetables from the third shelf. You will need to access all three shelves for just about any meal. While logical cohesion may help one find an item or subcomponent, the items or subcomponents do not work together for a single purpose.

We see logical cohesion in utility classes like IO classes or math libraries. Consider a math library. It may have a method to calculate square roots, methods for trigonometric functions and maybe radix conversion. Few programs will use all of these methods for a single functional reason. So the math library has a weak, merely logical cohesion.

Temporal Cohesion

As the name suggests, temporal (which means time-related) cohesive modules are those modules whose subcomponents reflect usage at about the same time. As an illustration, imagine another niche in a kitchen, such as a shelf or cupboard, by the garage door. On this shelf we might find a set of keys, a wallet or purse, a jacket and some sunglasses. What do these things have in common? These are all things that a person grabs as they head out the door to go somewhere. These are all things a person grabs at the same time and the person has chosen to keep them together so that in the event of going somewhere, it is easily convenient to access the items. Other than that, the items really have distant relationships.

In software, temporal relationships often occur near the beginning or ending of programs. Imagine a program that, before it closes, must deallocate some shared memory, close a file and close a transaction. If a programmer were to move these functions into a single method, the method would be temporally cohesive. Like logical cohesion, this organization has little to do with the function of the method and more to do with an easy way to categorize the functions.

Procedural Cohesion

At first blush, procedural cohesion appears to be very similar to temporal cohesion. With procedural cohesion programmers combine elements that the program uses to perform some process. Imagine a cupboard that contains a wire brush, charcoal, lighter fluid, matches, and a spatula. Backyard cooks will recognize these items as the items they use in the process of barbequing. These items are together because when a cook barbeques, the cook uses the same steps to prepare the fire and cook. The difference between procedural and temporal cohesion is that procedural cohesion is based on steps of a process whereas temporal cohesion is based on when these happen. Since process steps have a high correlation to timing, the two cohesions become blurred.

In software, an example of procedural cohesion might result from a process that requires checking authorization before allowing access to a resource such as a database. If a developer combines the steps of checking authorization followed by accessing a database into a module such as a method, then the method would have procedural cohesion.

Communicational Cohesion

Communicational cohesion is actually a very good form of cohesion even though it is not completely at the end of the cohesion spectrum. One might even argue that communicational cohesion is superior to sequential cohesion (which is next on the list). Communicational cohesion occurs when subcomponents of a module operate on the same data. Consider a bicycle tire repair kit. The kit contains patches, adhesive and tools for preparing the inner tube and applying the patches as well as a pump for inflating the tire. Each of these items works on the bicycle tire in a cohesive way.

In software, an example of communicational cohesion might be a class that contains all the CRUD (i.e., Create, Read, Update, Delete) functions for a database record. Each of these methods works together on the same data. To understand the strength of communicational cohesion, consider what happens when the database record contents or format changes. Only the module in question needs to change – and each method on that module will likely change. However, software that relies on this module may not be affected at all. This locality of change is a symptom of strong cohesion.

Sequential Cohesion

Sequential cohesion occurs when the components of a module link together in such a way that the output of one component becomes the input for the next component. As a somewhat humorous example of sequential cohesion, consider a Rube Goldberg-like machine to sharpen a pencil. The machine starts with a string tied to a kite. When the wind blows, the kite pulls the string, which is tied to the door of a cage full of moths. When the string opens the door and lets the moths out, they eat a nearby coat. The coat is attached to a pulley system such that as the coat gets lighter, the pulley lets a boot on the other end of the pulley drop. As the boot drops it turns on an electric switch that powers an electric iron. The iron burns a cat, inducing the cat to jump into a basket. The basket is attached to a pulley system so that as the basket goes down from the weight of the cat, the other end of the pulley, which is attached to a birdcage, raises and releases a woodpecker. When the woodpecker is released, the woodpecker starts to peck at a stick that is attached to knife. As the woodpecker pecks, the knife moves back and forth against the pencil sharpening it. Each component of the system works together in such a way that the output of one component becomes the input to the next. Undoubtedly, this is an extreme example, but it vividly illustrates the principle.

In software, an example of sequential cohesion might include a Linux shell command where the command consists of several programs tied together with pipes. Pipes in Linux tie the standard output of one program to the standard input of the next. For example, the first program in the command types the contents of a text file to standard output. The next program counts the number of words on each line and outputs a list of numbers representing the words count for each line. The third program might read in a list of numbers and calculate the average. The entire process calculates the average number of words per line of a text document.

Functional Cohesion

Functional cohesion means that all the subcomponents of a module contribute to a single well-defined task. Think about a dragster. Every piece of a dragster contributes to making the car move as fast to the finish line as possible. Compare a dragster to an average car. Notice that the dragster has no air conditioning, no luggage rack, no stereo and no cup holders. While these features may be helpful for a car that has multiple functions, they do not contribute to the single purpose of the dragster.

A software example of functional cohesion might be a stack abstraction with methods to push, pop and determine if the stack is empty. Each of these methods contributes to the function of the stack. Notice that a pure stack does not have ways to add values to the bottom or middle of the stack. Those methods would better suit a list. A pure stack with only the three basic methods performs with perfect functional cohesion.

Check Your Cohesion Intuition

It can be tricky to figure out what type of cohesion a software module has. So, to develop our cohesion intuition, let's work through some examples. Consider the following modules and try and classify what type of cohesion they each employ.

Module 1

```
void static main(String[] args) {

   setUpForProcessing();
   ...
   tearDownFromProcessing();
}

void setUpForProcessing() {
   getTheDBConnection();
   authorizeTheUser();
   openAllFiles();
   getEncryptionKey();
}

void tearDownFromProcessing() {
   closeAllFiles();
   releaseTheDBConnection();
}
```

Module 2

```
Dog createDog(String dogName) {
   ...
}

void updateDog(Dog dog) {
   ...
}

Dog getDog(String dogName) {
   ...
}

void deleteDog(String dogName) {
   ...
}
```

Module 3

```
class Utilities {

   int hashString(String str) {
      ...
   }

   int generateRandomInteger() {
      ...
   }

   void displayLogo() {
      ...
   }
}
```

Module 4

```
void static main(String[] args) {

   setUpConnection();
   issueServerRequest();
   ...
   setUpConnection();
   issueNextServerRequest();
   ...
   setUpConnection();
   issueFinalServerRequest();
}

void setUpConnection() {
   openTheSocket();
   sendTheProtocolPrelude();
   authenticateTheUser();
}
```

Module 5

```
class Queue {
   void addToEnd(Object object) {
      ...
   }
   Object removeFromFront() {
      ...
   }
   int getLength() {
      ...
   }
}
```

Module 6

```
class StringUtilities {

   String getReverse(String string) {
      ...
   }

   String getCamelCase(String string) {
      ...
   }

   String getRandomOrder(String string) {
      ...
   }
}
```

Module 7

```
String createMessagePacket(String message) {

    String envelope =
                addMessageEnvelope(message);
    String proto = encodeForProtocol(envelope);
    String cypher = encrypt(proto);

    Return cypher;
}
```

The following section discusses the intended classification for each module and explains the rationale for its classification. Write your answers down before you proceed so you can refer back to your answers and compare them to those in the discussion.

Classifying module cohesion can be confusing as the differences between modules can be very subtle. It is probably less useful to worry about the exact classification of the module and more important to get the general vicinity of the classification correct. However, here is the rationale for the classifications of the example modules.

Module 1 employs temporal cohesion. Temporal cohesion is difficult to distinguish from procedural cohesion since consecutive steps of a process occur close to each other in time. So how can we determine that Module 1 uses temporal cohesion and not procedural cohesion? The secret is to look at the steps of the methods setUpForProcessing() and tearDownFromProcessing(). These steps happen at the same time but could be in any order. For a module to employ procedural cohesion, the steps of the process must occur in process order. Since Module 1 combines several steps because they happen at the same time, we classify the module as temporally cohesive.

Module 2 employs communicational cohesion. This is apparent because the methods perform standard CRUD operations each working on the Dog class. Remember that the definition of communicational cohesion is that each member of the module works on common data.

Module 3 uses coincidental cohesion. Notice that none of the methods really have much to do with each other except that they are utilities that don't seem to belong anywhere else. The complete lack of relevance between the utilities means that we should classify the module as coincidental cohesion.

Module 4 is procedural cohesion. Notice that unlike module 1, the steps of the method of module 4 must be in order. This is how we can distinguish between procedural and temporal cohesion. Also, procedural cohesion may be difficult to distinguish from sequential cohesion. The major difference is that the steps of procedural cohesion must be in order, similar to sequential cohesion, however with procedural cohesion, the output from one step is not necessarily the input to the next step. This is the case with Module 4, so we classify module 4 as procedural cohesion.

Module 5 is functional cohesion. This is a nice tight class that has methods that only relate to what it does – no more and no less. Also notice that the class has only one purpose, which is to store objects in first-in-first-out order. Functional cohesion is what all modules strive for.

Module 6 uses logical cohesion. You might almost guess that module 6 is coincidental cohesion, but the difference is that the methods of this module have something in common – they all operate on strings. However, users of this module will seldom use more than one method at a time. The methods really don't *work* together. Therefore, Module 6 uses logical cohesion.

Module 7 employs sequential cohesion. Notice that, unlike procedural cohesion, the output from one step in the process is the input to the next. While sequential cohesion is similar to procedural cohesion, the chaining of the output to input classifies Module 7 as sequential cohesion.

Computer Science

Over the last few decades, computer scientists have been faced with a multitude of challenging problems of various sizes and shapes. As computer scientists have worked to meet these challenges, they have developed data structures and algorithms with distinct functionality and performance characteristics. By analyzing the functionality and performance characteristics of the data structures and algorithms, computer scientists have been able to identify preferred ways of delivering the functionality and performance required by each situation.

The results of responding to these challenges are a set of standard data structures and algorithms that become building blocks for more complex problems. For example, consider a common Most-Recently Used (MRU) caching mechanism. This mechanism tries to provide quick access to items that are most used by keeping those most recently used items in an area with optimal retrieval characteristics. Cache builders could start from scratch and build a custom set of data structures for this purpose, but the result would be complicated software that is expensive to develop. Instead, cache designers can use existing building blocks like a simple doubly linked list and an indexing hash table to construct the cache. By starting with existing constructs, developers can minimize defects, since they have already tested the constructs. Also, by reusing existing constructs developers reduce production time.

It is important for software developers to understand Computer Science so as to choose the most appropriate data structures and algorithms. Selecting the most appropriate constructs will provide developers with the necessary functionality and the optimal performance. When software uses the wrong constructs, attaining the necessary functionality becomes unnecessarily complicated and the performance often suffers. Therefore, developers must be familiar with common data structures and algorithms and apply them adroitly.

Coupling

Coupling deals with interactions between modules and the extent to which modules rely on each other. One way to think about coupling is to consider how independently reusable a module is. Modules that may be easily and independently reused with little complications are loosely coupled (desirable). Modules that can only be reused by also using associated modules are tightly coupled (undesirable).

Like cohesion, Larry Constantine also identified coupling as a design principle. Constantine describes coupling as a continuum with eight identifiable points along the continuum:
- Content coupling
- Common coupling
- External coupling
- Control coupling
- Stamp coupling
- Data coupling
- Message coupling
- No coupling

The following subsections explain each of these coupling instances.

Content Coupling

Content coupling occurs when one module relies on the internal constructs and operation of another module. As an example, imagine a vending machine for soda pop where the cans get stuck periodically. The owner of the machine might investigate how the machine works and realize that as cans stack up, a can gets lodged in the racks. So if a person knows how many cans are in the rack when a can gets stuck, the person can determine where to whack the machine on the side to cause the can to dislodge. Customers of other vending machines don't need to know how the machine works to use them, but customers of this jamming machine would need to know how the machine works in order to know how to make the machine work when cans get stuck.

Likewise some software modules might need to know how another module works to interact with the module. Imagine a stack abstraction that does not provide a method to determine how many items are on the stack. A module that uses the stack and requires this information would need to know how the stack works in order to calculate the number of items on the stack.

The problem with content coupling is that it is not possible to modify the dependent module without considering the depending software. For example, if the vending machine above changes so that cans still get stuck, but the cans get stuck for a different reason, all customers of the vending machine would need to be aware of the change in order to successfully use the machine.

Common Coupling

Common coupling means that two or more modules rely on a common (global) resource. Consider teenagers in a household who share a common car. In order for the teenagers to successfully use the car, they must keep other members of the household aware of the effects of their car use. For example, the young drivers would need to let each other know who plans to use the car when, where they left the car and how much gas is in the car. Imagine the frustration of one of the drivers when the driver needs the car for an urgent trip and gets in the car only to find the other driver has left the gas tank empty.

Similarly with software, when two or more modules share common data, the modules must coordinate carefully. Since there are no restrictions on which modules can use the data, if a module finds the data in an invalid state, it becomes very difficult to determine the culprit and fix the problem.

External Coupling

External coupling exists when multiple modules rely on a common external protocol or format. If two or more spies share a secret code that allows them to communicate, consider the problems that occur if the code is compromised and needs to change. All parties using the code need to stop using the current code and switch over to a new code all at the same time.

Similarly, think about the HTML protocol and how it links web servers with web browsers. Now imagine that somebody wants to introduce, or even worse, remove a feature from HTML. The suppliers of all browsers would need to change their browsers. Simultaneously all web servers also need to be updated. This is such a huge problem, that we seldom see changes to HTML itself. Instead, we use JavaScript to add functionality and to work around the limitations of HTML.

External coupling is different from common coupling in that external coupling relies on a global definition. Common coupling relies on global data. However, both of these forms of coupling rely on global resources.

Control Coupling

Control coupling happens when a calling module A, passes another module B, a parameter that specifically changes the flow of execution in module B. To illustrate control coupling, think about a company that does mobile phone repair. The repair company has two divisions; one that does iPhone repairs and another that does Android phone repairs. The company has customers fill out a form they send along with their phone to the company headquarters. One of the fields on the form is the address of the division that will actually be doing the repairs. When workers at the company headquarters receive a phone for repair, they look at the form and then mail the phone to the division's address on the form. This example illustrates the useless extra step customers need to go through since customers could just as easily mail the phone directly to the appropriate division.

An example of control coupling in software might occur in a robotics control module that controls a robot motor. The motor can move either forward or backward. Control coupling would exist if the robot control module has a single method named "move(Direction d)" with a parameter explaining the direction. The module could eliminate the control coupling by replacing the single method with two methods (each with no parameters), named "moveForward()" and "moveBackward()" thereby eliminating the control parameter. Since the calling software already knows which direction to move the motor, it makes more sense for the calling method to specify the direction directly in the method name instead of encoding it in a parameter that the called module must then inspect.

Stamp Coupling

Stamp coupling occurs when software passes heavyweight structures to modules that only use a portion of the structure's contents. Imagine a backpacker that doesn't like to repack his/her backpack. So instead of packing only those items needed for a specific trip, the backpacker packs everything he/she might need on any backpacking trip. These things might include climbing ropes, raft trip life-vests, hunting equipment and extra parkas and winter clothing. Now, if the backpacker is headed out for a few days in the desert in the mid summer, he/she will be carrying a lot of extra weight with no apparent benefit other than the backpacker is too lazy to repack.

A software example of this happens when web developers use a single global object to handle session information. The session object might contain the user's name, the shopping cart contents, the user's account history and user preferences. Because it seems convenient, the software passes the session object to any module that requires any of the items in the session object. This has two affects; first, it is not clear to readers of the code which items are useful for any given operation, and second, if the software inadvertently changes one of the items in the session object, it requires significant effort to narrow down where the inadvertent change occurred.

Data Coupling

Data coupling means that a module uses simple parameters. The types of the parameters are such that the module completely consumes the parameter with no unused portions of parameters. As an example, imagine a chair assembler. Each assembled chair consists of four legs a seat and a back, so to get an assembled chair, one sends exactly four legs a seat and a back, and the assembler produces the chair. The assembler needs no additional parts such as tables or office supplies. These additional parts would only clutter the assembler's workspace and confuse the assembler.

Basic math functions are great examples of data coupling. For example, consider the power function. This function receives a base number and an exponent and produces the result. The parameters are basic types and the function requires no additional information.

Message Coupling

A module has message coupling if its method have no parameters – just simple commands. Consider a simple robotic tank with a voice command interface where the only commands the tank understands are move, stop, turn left, turn right, stop turning and fire. One can fully control the tank with these commands and each command requires no parameters.

Message coupled software works the same way. Think about the administrative interface for a print server. The server might have methods to start the service, stop the service, put the service online and put the service offline. None of these methods require any parameters – merely their invocation is enough to trigger the functionality.

No Coupling

While the designation of "no coupling" is practically not very useful, completeness requires that we mention it. Modules are not coupled if they have no interaction because they are completely unrelated. For example, Rovio's "Angry Birds" game has no coupling to Windows Solitaire game. While the distinction is not very helpful, it suggests an extreme case in which either of the two games could be changed without consideration of the other. This is a theoretical limit in coupling.

Direct Expression

The principle of direct expression stipulates that software source code should use the most straightforward way of stating its purpose. There are often many ways of performing a task in software; however, some ways are more obvious than others. All things being equal, the principle of direct expression suggests using the most obvious.

Sometimes software developers employ circuitous approaches. There may be any number of reasons for this. Developers may be constrained by some resource and may have chosen an obscure approach to circumvent the resource constraint. Or, a developer may have chosen an approach because of a predisposition based on previous experience or because the developer has not fully conceptualized the problem. Additionally, a developer may just want to show off something they think is interesting or "looks cool". Whenever functionally possible, developers should avoid these clever tricks and approaches in favor of approaches that are more straightforward.

Examples of obscure approaches include, but are not limited to:
- Using bit shifting to multiply by a power of two
- Over using operator overloading where it doesn't naturally apply
- Using strings instead of creating or using a more appropriate data type
- Using iteration when the solution is naturally recursive
- Over-engineering for unwarranted scalability, etc.

- Relying on any obscure side effect from a process or calculation
- Overlooking natural loops

Limit Interaction

Limiting interaction is about designing software so that developers don't have to think about too many pieces at any one time. Studies have shown that the average human mind easily can remember seven things give or take a couple. Large-scale software systems obviously contain many more things than seven, so it is necessary to structure software so that developers can navigate the system's complexity, understand its every detail and not be overwhelmed.

Many novice developers have had the experience of building software with challenging complexity. Often, as developers attack the software development, they get to a point where one more detail or complexity suddenly becomes overwhelming to the point where the developer considers giving up. Analysis of these situations usually shows that there was no single complexity or quantum of detail that brought the developer to his/her knees, but instead it is the steady aggregation of all the details.

Since there is no single major offender in this proverbial straw that broke the camel's back, it is important to manage each minor piece of complexity so as not to arrive at the point of overwhelming despair. Developers can do this by paying attention to each minor piece of detail and eliminating unnecessary complexity no matter how minor it may appear.

A major source of complexity results from having to consider the relationships between software constructs such as operators and operands. As the number of constructs that require consideration grows, the number of relationships between those constructs grows in a combinatorial fashion. Therefore, it is critical to limit each additional construct.

Metaphor

The principle of metaphor allows developers to relate a software system with which they are not familiar to a more familiar system. Software systems have rich and complex relationships. Understanding all the relationships and intricacies can take significant time and effort. Developers can reduce the cost of understanding a system quickly by identifying the similarities between systems.

The easiest way to create a metaphor is to use names that suggest the role that constructs, such as operators and operands, play within a system. For example, a model of a chess game might have a class that contains all the pieces of the same color. By naming this class "Team", we conjure up an immediate understanding of what the class does. The name "Team" suggested that we might expect methods to determine piece membership, we might anticipate being able to get a roster and we might also anticipate multiple instances of the class since games usually involve multiple teams. Quickly understanding all these relationships and complexities results from the simple choice of a useful mnemonic.

Notice that the use of metaphor in terms of naming is nearly second nature. However, in some cases the reflex of metaphor seems to break down. There are several reasons for these breakdowns. Sometimes developers don't stop to think about a construct long enough to consider its relationships and choose a useful name. Other times the names developers choose might not be general enough to allow the metaphor to work.

While metaphor can be a very helpful tool in explaining software, misusing metaphor can be very harmful. For example, if a developer chooses a name that misrepresents a construct, someone trying to understand the code will travel down a blind alley. The reader of the code must come to a deep enough understanding of the system so as to debunk the misdirecting metaphor. This can take much more effort than had the original developer used no metaphor at all! Therefore, metaphor must be used carefully and with skill.

Normalization

Normalization is the concept of reducing a representation of a concept to its fundamental expression, or in other words, eliminating redundancy. For decades, database designers have understood the necessity of normalizing data by designing database schemas so that database tables represent each data item in only one location. Traditionally students of database design and data modeling learn of first normal form, second normal form, etc. These forms represent rules for transforming schemas by removing redundancy.

The value of database normalization lies in its reduced conceptual load. Compare updating a normalized database to a non-normalized database. In a non-normalized database, data updates may have to change several data values across several tables. This requires the software developers to wrap their minds around the table structure and its intricacies so as to remember everything that they must change to affect the update. This effort is similar to the conceptual load necessary for conjugating an irregular verb versus a regular verb.

While database designers commonly apply normalization to database schemas, software developers apply these same principles when formulating data models using memory-based data structures. Sound designs demonstrate normalization of data within classes, lists and hash tables. Sometimes these in-memory data structures map to database tables, but sometimes there is no mapping to a corresponding database. Normalization has more to do with the relationships between the data and little to do with the address space housing the data.

Similarly, developers can also normalize program control flow. In software development, the antithesis of normalized control flow occurs when developers copy and paste sections of code instead of introducing methods to extract and isolate unique control flows. While it may require a bit more mental effort upfront to eliminate the redundancy, the overall conceptual load that results from the normalization frees up the developers' cognitive processing for other design conceptualization. This is significant for designing software at scale.

Orthodoxy

The word *Orthodox* means adherence to accepted norms. Orthodoxy, in software development, means using common practices. Over the history of software development, developers have converged on some common development practices. These practices have withstood the test of time because they offer some value and are usually based on sound design principles.

For example, developers have created the practice of using getter and setter methods to access fields within a class. These methods provide a level of indirection that separates the access of the data from the representation of the data. This separation allows developers to change the representation of the data without affecting those who use the getters and setters.

Those uninitiated to the practice of using getters and setters may find this an odd practice. After all, how often does software really take advantage of this indirection? Those who espouse an agile philosophy might be inclined to suggest not using getters and setters until the software demonstrates the need for the indirection. However, developers have grown accustomed to this practice and expect to see the getters and setters. When seasoned developers do not see these methods, the conceptual load imposed on the developers to try and figure out why the getters and setter do not exist outweighs the cost of providing the getters and setters.

Orthodoxy is about being predictable. Often, a person who is an inexperienced driver will approach traffic situations without awareness of traffic norms. The result is unexpected behavior. For example, an inexperienced driver might cut diagonally across stalls in a parking lot and take the most direct route to the exit of the lot. Experienced drivers don't expect other drivers to be crossing diagonally through the lot and may not think to look out for such drivers.

Similarly, software developers anticipate orthodox behavior. Deviations from anticipated behavior may be completely functional, but can increase conceptual load since the unorthodox behavior requires those steeped in the practice to have to understand the intent and look for any special circumstances that may apply. Imagine reading some unorthodox code and asking yourself, "Why did the developer build the software this way instead of the normal way? Is there something I'm missing here?" This is like a speed bump for the reader of the software.

Having preached the value of orthodoxy, it is also necessary to add a note of caution. Sometimes people develop norms that are not founded on sound principles, or due to industry progress the norms no longer apply. For example, some of the development practices involving software documentation that were helpful before developers had powerful integrated development environments (IDEs) don't make sense in today's environment. Developers should analyze norms from time to time to make sure the norms still makes sense. However, before abandoning a time-tested practice, it is important to fully understand what value the practice had originally provided.

Chapter 3 - The Mechanics of Refactoring

Imagine yourself working on a development team where one of the members has recently left the team. You have been assigned responsibility for the exiting developer's code. You decide to familiarize yourself with the code so that you will be prepared to make any necessary changes, so you sit down and start to peruse the code.

To your dismay you realize that the developer has used many techniques and approaches that are not up to your principled standards. Your manager has given you some time to get up to speed on this code and you decide you want to start cleaning it up. How should you proceed?

The number one rule in refactoring is: do no harm. This means that whatever changes you make, you must not change the code so that it no longer works. While it seems obvious that the code should continue to work, it is not always obvious what *works* means. For example, if the code you inherited would throw an exception for certain parameter values, is that a bug or a feature?

In order to assure that you do not break the code, you must first understand exactly what the code is supposed to do. We refer to statements defining what the code should do as *requirements statements*. The easiest way to recognize requirements statements is that requirements statements generally complete the sentence "The system should…"

However, true requirements statements must do a little more than explain what a system should do. In addition, requirements statements must be measurable. For example, a statement like "The system should fly high" is not a true requirement statement because the *high* attribute is not constrained – in other words we don't know how high the system should fly. We can refer to unconstrained statements that sound like requirements as *preferences*.

Once we are able to articulate exactly what the system should do (in this case the system is the software we have inherited), we are able to assure that we don't break the system as we refactor. However, it is probably important to put a safety net in place to make sure that we do not inadvertently break the system. This safety net comes in the form of regression tests that make sure the system continues to fulfill its requirements. Should we accidentally introduce a flaw into the system, our regression tests will alert us to our mistake.

It is important to put the regression tests together before changing any of the code. The regression tests prove that the original code complies with the requirements. Without these regression tests, if you notice that the system seems not to be functioning correctly, you can't be sure if the problem is one you introduced or if the problem existed in the original code.

Another important aspect of regression tests is that you can run them without significant human interaction. This makes the tests easy and relatively quick to run, which in turn allows you to run the tests frequently. It is important to run your regression tests often so you can get immediate feedback on the effects of your changes. Immediate feedback helps you isolate which changes have affected the behavior of the system.

If no tests exist for the original system, or if you suspect that the tests are not very complete, how do you go about figuring out how to test the target system? Many developers will sit around and daydream about different things they might throw at the system. Others consider testing to be an art form where testing artists have an innate flair for identifying good tests. Still others believe that it is impossible to test your own code since you have a mindset that prevents you from being thorough. None of these perspectives is very helpful. If testing is an art form or performed by those who daydream up tests, how can you know if your code has been well tested? Who is to say that the code is well tested, or instead, that the test artist just happened to have limited imagination for this particular code? And if you can't test your own code, then you will need to wait for one of these testing artists to become available and willing to help you.

What you need is a process that will allow you to identify and enumerate the tests you should use so you can have confidence that your code fulfills the requirements. If such a process did exist, then all you would need to do to test your code would be to follow the process.

Such a process does exist. There are two main principles that drive the process; the first principle is to try to make sure the system does the right things, and the second principle is to make sure the system does things right. While the grammar of the previous sentence is not quite correct, the sentence is helpful in remembering the principles. To identify the necessary tests for your code, use each of these principles.

The first principle of *doing the right thing* means that you identify tests by focusing on the requirements. Remember, we said that requirements must be constrained, or in other words, requirements must have measurable boundaries. Start to identify your test cases by trying things that explore the boundaries specified in the requirements. For example, if your system should add two 16-bit signed integer values (which is the requirement), your tests should try various values around the boundaries of the requirement. These boundaries would include the maximum and minimum integer values of 65,535 and -65,536. You should also consider other boundaries in the values like 0, 1 and -1. You may also want to throw in a couple of examples of values in the middle, say 32,767 and -32,767. Once you have tried all of these boundaries, you can have some reasonable confidence that your system meets the requirements and that you have all the necessary code in your system.

36

Whereas the first principle, *doing the right thing*, assures that you have all the necessary code in your system, the second principle of *doing the thing right* tries to make sure that all the code works as expected. You do this by looking at the code itself. What you are trying to do is make sure that your tests execute all possible code pieces. You may want to use a code coverage tool to help you identify what code your tests do and do not execute.

Start by running the tests you created using the first principle and determine which lines of code the tests do not exercise. Next, construct additional tests that cause the unexecuted sections of the program to be exercised. Verify that the tests also produce the expected results.

It may be helpful to think about the code in terms of condition coverage, or which conditions in the code the tests exercise. If your tests cause each condition in the code to result in true and false, then you can be assured that your tests exercise all the code because the tests execute all the branches. Note that some branches depend on a compound of conditions (e.g., tests that have ANDs and ORs), so it is not sufficient to simply have each branch be true or false. You must also make sure that you test each condition in a branch for a true value and a false value.

Once you have written tests that explore the boundaries of the requirements and exercise all the code, you can be reasonably confident that the code works and that your testing of that piece is complete. It is not necessary to spend hours staring at the ceiling thinking about other strange things that you might try. Your safety net is in place and you can actually start to make changes to the code – rerunning the tests after each change.

For object-oriented code, there are a few more considerations relating to the mechanics of testing. Most current object-oriented languages such as Java or C# have testing frameworks. These testing frameworks let developers create test methods that perform operations and make assertions about the state of the code. Most developers create test procedures that perform some operation and then the test procedure asserts some condition that shows that the operation was successful. You can make your tests more robust if you let the test procedures start by asserting the precondition for the test. For example, if you are testing a sort method for sorting a list, start the test by asserting that the list is not in sorted order. After calling the sort method, then assert that the list *is* in sorted order. In this way the test procedure proves that the sort method has had the desired affect on the list. Asserting the preconditions of the test makes sure the test indeed tests what you intend.

The target of a set of test cases may be the methods of an object that manipulate some data or state that is only accessible by using other methods of the object. This can cause a bit of a testing dilemma since you don't know if the methods are making the necessary modifications to the data or state without using other untested methods to access the object's data or state. Some developers have tried to circumvent the object by making private data public or by writing some other mechanism to access the state of the object. Neither of these approaches is desirable since they require basically rewriting the class, or leaving object state exposed. The way to solve this chicken/egg problem is to focus each test case on a single specific method. Then assume that this target method of focus is suspect, but all other methods of the class work correctly. Test each method of the class, one-by-one, in this manner. While logically this seems like circular reasoning, in practice this approach works very well.

One final piece of advice in formulating test methods; make sure each test method can run independently of the other test methods. This requires that each test case perform the necessary initialization and cleanup. If multiple test cases require the same setup and/or cleanup, the setup or cleanup may be abstracted into another method that all those test cases may use. The value of having independent test cases is that you can run them in any order and you won't be confused or misled by leftover side effects.

Building adequate testing requires some effort. The result is a set of test software that has value. It is important to treat this supporting test software with as much care as you would your production code. Be sure to use a revision control system to keep the tests in sync with the source code. Don't let test cases become dilapidated. As tests start to fail because they are out of date with the current requirements, the test cases exhibit false positive results. Like calling wolf, these false positives can cause developers not to trust the test suite and to start to ignore the results. Once this begins to happen it becomes harder and harder to ever get the tests back up to snuff. Therefore, use discipline to keep the tests current.

When you realize the cost of maintaining a current test suite you may be tempted to jettison the test suite. Be very thoughtful before making this decision. Fundamentally testing is a risk/reward proposition. If you do not perform tests, you may save the costs of the test development, but you will incur the risk that the software will not work at some critical juncture. These risks have a way of catching up to you at the most inopportune times – such as the holiday season when you can ill-afford to have your ecommerce server go down because of a bug. To some extent, testing is often one of those pay-me-now or pay-me-later situations. However, when you jostle code around, you are likely to break it, and there are few things that jostle code around more than refactoring. So taking the time to put tests in place before you begin refactoring is a high reward bet.

Chapter 4 – Cohesion-Based Rules

The principle of cohesion deals with how integrated a component is. Cohesion significantly influences the rules in this chapter. While refactoring rules may have many influencing principles, the rules in this chapter relate more directly to cohesion.

Extract Class

Abstract

When one class seems to be doing more than one thing, consider creating an additional class so that each class has only one responsibility.

Discussion

When a class has a single responsibility, it is easy to conceptualize, to test and to maintain. If you feel like a class is doing more than one thing, you may have overlooked an abstraction. Try to articulate what the overlooked class is by considering the responsibilities of the bloated class. Extract each separate responsibility of the bloated class into its own class [Cohesion].

There are two major forms of this rule; the first form results in classes that are peers to one another. In this case, the original bloated class and its new sibling class both provide functionality to a third class; the methods of the original class separate into the two sibling classes with very little dissection of the methods. The second form results in classes with a client/server relationship. The original class usually serves as a client that uses services of the new class.

Example 1

Here is an example of a class that performs two responsibilities that can be separated into two sibling classes. The original bloated class keeps track of operations on a stack for do/undo functionality. The bloated class also parses commands into operations. The original class has logical cohesion. Refactoring the bloated class into a class that stacks operations and a second class that parses commands into operations yields two classes with functional cohesion.

Before:

```
class CommandHandler {

    void pushOperation(Operation operation) {
        ...
    }

    Operations popOperation() {
        ...
    }

    boolean hasOperations() {
        ...
    }

    Operation parseCommand(String command) {
        ...
    }
}
```

After:

```
class OperationStack {

    void pushOperation(Operation operation) {
        ...
    }

    Operations popOperation() {
        ...
    }

    boolean hasOperations() {
        ...
    }

}

class CommandParser {

    Operation parseCommand(String command) {
        ...
    }
}
```

Example 2

In this example, the bloated class contains a subordinate abstraction. The bloated class is a Person class that keeps track of each of the parts of a phone number. These parts fit nicely into a phone number abstraction, which the Person class can use.

Before:

```
class Person {

   String getAreaCode() {
      ...
   }
   String getPhoneNumber() {
      ...
   }
}
```

After:

```
class PhoneNumber {

   String getAreaCode() {
      ...
   }
   String getNumber() {
      ...
   }
}

class Person {

   PhoneNumber getPhoneNumber() {
      ...
   }
}
```

Extract Subclass

Abstract

A class has behaviors and/or fields that only some instances use. This may be an indication that you need to create a subclass for the subset of constructs.

Discussion

Developers should follow design intuition based on a sound understanding of cohesion when they create classes or subclasses. However, sometimes we can help develop our design intuition. This rule is an indication that our intuition may have overlooked an abstraction. Identify the features that likely belong in the overlooked subclass and see if you can articulate a name for the subclass. Quite often if you can name the subclass with a useful name [Metaphor], it is a good indication that you should realize the abstraction. Conversely, if you have trouble finding a non-bogus name for the abstraction, then the abstraction may not be a useful one [Cohesion].

Example

In this example, the JobItem class has three methods; getTotalPrice(), getUnitPrice() and getEmployee(). However, only a few of the JobItems actually use the getEmployee() method. Further inspection reveals that those JobItems that use the getEmployee() method are items that relate to a service as opposed to a product. Therefore, it makes sense to extract the getEmployee() method into a ServiceItem class which is a JobItem. The refactored code shows this extraction.

Before:

```
class JobItem  {

  Decimal getUnitPrice() {
    ...
  }

  Decimal getTotalPrice() {
    ...
  }

  Decimal getEmployee() {
    ...
  }
}
```

After:

```
class JobItem  {

  Decimal getUnitPrice() {
    ...
  }

  Decimal getTotalPrice() {
    ...
  }
}

class ServiceItem extends JobItem {

  Decimal getEmployee() {
    ...
  }
}
```

Extract Superclass

Abstract

Two or more classes have similar methods or fields. Create a superclass and move the common constructs into the superclass.

Discussion

Good design intuition based on principles of cohesion will usually uncover superclass abstractions. However, if you find you have several classes with common fields and/or methods, it is possible you have overlooked a superclass abstraction. Consider creating a superclass and moving the common constructs into the superclass [Normalization]. However, before doing so, check to make sure you can give a useful name to the superclass [Metaphor]. Also, make sure that each of the subclasses has a valid "is-a" relationship with the new superclass. If you cannot find a useful name for the superclass, or the subclasses do not have a true "is-a" relationship with the superclass, you may not want to create the superclass since it appears not to be a valid abstraction [Cohesion].

Example

Here is an example of two classes that both have a getName() method. Upon further inspection we realize that both classes represent cartoon characters. Since we are able to articulate the name of the superclass (i.e., Character) and since all cartoon characters have names, it makes sense to refactor the getName() method into a Character class. The refactored code shows the result. Notice that the Character class passes the test that its subclasses have an "is-a" relationship.

Before:

```
class Flintstone {
   String getName() {
      …
   }
}

class Jetson {
   String getName() {
      …
   }
}
```

After:

```
class Character {
   String getName() {
      …
   }
}

class Flintstone extends Character {
}

class Jetson extends Character {
}
```

Move Field

Abstract

One class uses another class's field more than the class containing the field. Consider moving the field to the other class.

Discussion

Like the *Move Method* rule, when a class uses a field contained in another class more than that containing class uses the field, it may be an indication that the field really belongs to the class that uses the field instead of the class containing the field. Consider moving the field [Cohesion, Coupling].

However, like the *Move Method* rule, you should move fields judiciously and only when sound design intuition suggests that the move will actually improve cohesion. If you are trying to develop or strengthen your design intuition, noticing that a non-containing class uses a field more than the containing class may be a symptom that you need to consider changing the class' abstraction.

You should never apply this rule if the field is logically part of the defining class' abstraction. By doing so and breaking the abstraction, you will probably end up moving the field back in the future because, as you add code, the new code will undoubtedly end up using the field in the original containing class.

Example

Here is an example of a field that is in the wrong class. The Dog class may use the mastersName field some, but it is clear that the name belongs to the Person class even if the Dog class uses the name more frequently.

Before:

```
class Dog {
   private String mastersName;

   String getMastersName() {
      Return mastersName;
   }
...
}

class Person {
   Dog pet;

   void someMethod(){
      ...
      print(pet.getMastersName() +
               "is my name");
      ...
   }
...
}
```

After:

```
class Dog {
   private Person master;
   ...
}

class Person {

   Dog pet;
   private String name;

   String getName() {
      Return name;
   }

   void someMethod(){
      ...
      print(name + "is my name");
      ...
   }
...
}
```

Move Method

Abstract

A method uses more of the resources on a class other than the one on which it is defined. Consider moving the method to the other class.

Discussion

If a method uses more of the fields and methods of one other class than the class on which it is defined, this may be an indicator that the method belongs to the other class. If this is the case, then you should move the method to the other class. However, the use of resources such as fields and methods is only an indicator – not proof that you may need to move the method. The acid test is the class' cohesion.

For example, a class may appear to use methods and fields from another class, but this may be because the system of classes is not yet fully mature. In time the balance may shift as the class containing the method becomes better defined.

Another reason that it may falsely appear necessary to move a method is if the fields of the other class are misplaced. Perhaps it may make more sense to move the field or fields from the other class to the class containing the method in question. Consider the effects of each of these modifications. Ultimately use cohesion to determine which resources should reside in which classes [Cohesion].

Example 1

This example illustrates a method that obviously should be moved from the Dog class to the Person class. The method uses more of the resources of the Person class and also the method fits better into the Person class from the perspective of cohesion.

Before:

```
class Dog {
...
   void printMaster() {
      println("Name:  " + master.getName());
      println("Address:  " +
                     master.getAddress());
   }
...
}
```

After:

```
class Person {
   private String name;
   private String address;
   ...
   void printDetails() {
      println("Name:  " + name);
      println("Address:  " + address);
   }
...
}
```

Example 2

Here is an example of a method that has indicators that the method should be moved, however, the class' cohesion would break down as a result of moving the method. The performMorningActivities method calls more methods on the dog class than anything else, but this method should not be moved to the Dog class. This method is logically cohesive with the Person class.

```
class Person {
   Dog dog = new Dog();
   …
   void performMorningActivities() {
      dog.walk();
      dog.feed();
      eatBreakfast();
      dog.pet();
   }
…
}
```

Push Down Construct

Abstract

A field or method on a superclass is only relevant to a subset of its subclasses. Move the construct to the subclasses.

Discussion

If a behavior or field in a superclass only applies to a subset of the subclasses, then you need to move the construct [Cohesion]. If the subset of subclasses contains only one subclass, move the construct to that class. If there are several subclasses in the subset, you may want to introduce a new subclass with the construct that acts as a superclass for all classes in the subset [Normalization].

Example

This example shows a Character class that has a getSpaceShip() method. Since Flintstones are stone age characters, Flintstones will never use the getSpaceShip() method. Therefore, refactoring moves the method to the Jetson class – which is the only class using the method.

Before:

```
class Character {
   SpaceShip getSpaceShip() {
      ...
   }
   ...
}

class Flintstone extends Character {

   ...
}

class Jetson extends Character {

   ...
}
```

After:

```
class Character {
   ...
}

class Flintstone extends Character {

   ...
}

class Jetson extends Character {

   ...
   SpaceShip getSpaceShip() {
      ...
   }
}
```

Separate Query from Modifier

Abstract

Code has a method that returns a value and modifies the state of the object. Create two new methods; one for the query and one for the modifications of the state.

Discussion

Methods, like classes, have a cohesive attribute. Methods should perform one conceptual task [Cohesion]. A method that queries the object for a value and also modifies the state of the object has two tasks. One downside of this dual-purpose method is that callers of the method may not be aware of the state modification. The upside of having two separate methods is that each of these methods is more likely to be reused.

The idea behind this rule applies to any method that performs more than one task. Combining multiple tasks is often a symptom of temporal cohesion. Developers can strengthen the cohesion by replacing the method with methods that perform the individual tasks. If the design calls for a method that combines the functionality of the individual methods, the calling method should strive for functional cohesion. The calling method will likely reside in a class outside (logically above) the class that contains the individual methods.

Example

This example shows a Stack class that has an odd method; removeTopItemAndGetResultingCount(). This method discards the top item from the stack and returns the number of items left on the stack. These types of methods sometimes are a result of a functional decomposition design process where the software designer requires certain functionality without considering the cohesion of the resulting abstraction. The refactored code separates the two functions into two methods.

Before:

```
class Stack {

    ...
    int removeTopItemAndGetResultingCount() {
        ...
    }
    ...
}
```

After:

```
class Stack {

    ...
    Object pop() {
        ...
    }

    int getCount() {
        ...
    }
    ...
}
```

Chapter 5 - Computer Science-Based Rules

Computer Science dictates using appropriate data structures and algorithms. Certain data structures and algorithms have specific characteristics, which suit them well for specific situations. While the rules in this chapter may have several foundational principles, these rules strongly illustrate the influence of the Computer Science principle.

Prefer Returning Iterators to Collections

Abstract

Methods that return collections instead of iterators require the method to construct the entire collection prior to returning. Use iterators to give the method the option to delay building the collection.

Discussion

Building a collection can be expensive – especially for large collections. Iterators provide a level of indirection so that the building of the collection may be delayed until the calling code actually dereferences the contents of the collection. For example, imagine a database query that returns a million results. If the code returns these results in a collection, the code will need to consume enough memory to contain all results. In addition, the code returning the collection will need to perform the processing to add each item to the results. Now imagine that the code querying the database only wants to consider the top 10 results. This scenario consumes wasteful amounts of memory and processing. On the other hand, an iterator might only consume enough memory and processing for each result - only as the querying code needs each result [Computer Science]. It is messy to mix code that works with collections and code that works with iterators. Therefore, prefer iterators to avoid the complication [Orthodoxy].

Example

Here the pre-refactored example shows a getMembers() method on an Organization class that returns a list of Person. Notice that this code has to construct the entire list based on the results of a query prior to returning. If there are lots of results, this method may have to do a lot of processing and consume significant amounts of memory.

The refactored version of the method returns an iterator of Person. The iterator allows the Organization class to construct the Person at the last instant and only if needed. For example, if the code calling getMembers() only uses the first few results, the remainder of the results will never be instantiated and the processing and memory will be conserved.

Before:

```
class Organization {

   List<Person> getMembers() {
      Query query = constructQuery();
      Results results = query.execute();
      ArrayList<Person> members =
         new ArrayList<Person>();
      for (Result result : results) {
         Person person =
            new Person(result.getItem());
         People.add(person);
      }
      return members;
   }
   ...
}
```

After:

```
class Organization {

   Iterator<Person> getMembers() {
      Query query = constructQuery();
      Results results = query.execute();
      PersonIterator iterator =
         new PersonIterator(results);
      return iterator;
   }
   ...
}

class PersonIterator implements Iterator {

   Results results;

   PersonIterator(Results results) {
      this.results = results;
   }

   boolean hasNext() {
      return reults.hasNext();
   }

   Object next() {
      Result result = (Result) results.next();
      return result.getItem();
   }

   void remove() {
      results.remove();
   }
}
```

Replace Algorithm

Abstract

Code uses an awkward algorithm that is difficult to understand. Replace the algorithm with a more straightforward algorithm.

Discussion

Sometimes as developers work to solve complicated problems they develop complex or convoluted algorithms. After a good night's sleep of after some reflection it may become apparent how to change the algorithm to make it much clearer how the algorithm works [Computer Science]. In this case, make the change.

Developers may resist changing algorithms for a number of reasons: they may not recognize a cleaner approach, they may be nervous to change something that was so difficult to build, or they may feel they have a personal investment in the algorithm because it took so long to develop. However, if there is an algorithm that does the same thing in a more understandable way [Direct Expression], developers should take an "egoless" approach and make the change.

Example

Here is an example of a method that searches for a person in the array that is a recognizable Flintstone character based on the person's name. Some might wonder if the replacing algorithm is really better – after all, it is more lines of code. Less code is not always better. In this case, the additional code affords the developer an additional cohesive method. Also, the replacing code uses a data table instead of a list of branching statements. The data table is preferable because the table can be modified easily with no duplication

[Normalization]. The table also is poised for resuse should the occasion arise.

Before:

```
boolean isFlintstoneCharacter(Person[] people)
{
   for (int i = 0; i < people.length; i++) {
      if (people[i].getName().equals("Fred"))
         return true;
      if (people[i].getName().equals("Wilma"))
         return true;
      if (people[i].getName().equals("Barney"))
         return true;
      if (people[i].getName().equals("Betty"))
         return true;
      if (people[i].getName().
                         equals("Mr. Slate"))
         return true;
   }
   return false;
}
```

After:

```java
boolean isFlintstoneCharacter(Person[] people)
{
   boolean found = false;
   for (int i = 0; !found &&
           (i < people.length); i++) {
      found = isFlintstoneName(
                   people[i].getName());
   }
   return found;
}

static final String[] flintstoneNames = {
   "Fred",
   "Wilma",
   "Barney",
   "Betty",
   "Mr. Slate"
};

boolean isFlintstoneName(String name) {
   boolean found = false;
   for (int i = 0; !found &&
        (i < flintsoneNames.length); i++) {
      found = name.equals(flintstoneNames[i]);
   }
   return found;
}
```

Replace Recursion with Iteration

Abstract

Sometimes code uses recursion where iteration is more
appropriate. Remove the recursion and use iteration instead.

Discussion

As developers finish building programs, they sometimes
realize that the entire program, or a major portion of a
program, should repeat itself. Rather than insert the repeating
portion into a loop, the developer recursively calls the
repeating portion of the code. This approach has several
problems. First of all, each time the program repeats the
section, the program consumes additional stack space to save
the context of the previous repetition. This context is no
longer useful. If the program repeats enough times, the
program will eventually run out of memory and crash.
Additionally, developers do not usually use this approach, so it
can require significant effort and time for those trying to
familiarize themselves with the program to make sense of
what is going on.

Using a loop in this situation works better because the loop
approach avoids the additional clutter on the stack [Limit
Interaction], more directly captures what the program is doing
[Direct Expression] and is the approach most developers
would anticipate [Orthodoxy].

While it is true that you can rewrite any recursive algorithm
using a loop, some algorithms naturally lend themselves to
recursion and some do not. To convert a naturally recursive
algorithm to use a loop, you use a stack to keep track of the
recursive context for later use (i.e., when returning up from the
recursion). To determine if an algorithm works better
recursively, try converting the algorithm to use a loop and see

if the algorithm requires a stack. If the algorithm does not require a stack, the algorithm is not naturally recursive and the loop works better. If the algorithm is not naturally recursive, prefer iteration to recursion [Computer Science].

Example

Here is an example of a computer game. When the game is over, the user may want to play the game again. The pre-refactored code repeats the game play using recursion. Notice that in doing so, the program stack must carry the context from the previous game play – which is never referenced. The refactored version of the game loops until the user no longer wants to play.

Before:

```
class Game {

    void play() {
        // Kill zombies here…

        if (userWantsToPlayAgain()) {
        Game game = new Game();
            play();
        }
    }

    static void main(String args[]) {

        Game game = new Game();
        Game.play();
    }
}
```

After:

```
class Game {

   void play() {
      // Kill zombies here…
   }

   static void main(String args[]) {

      do {
         Game game = new Game();
         Game.play();
      } while (userWantsToPlayAgain());
   }
}
```

Use Appropriate Data Types

Abstract

Code uses a data type that does not have the directly required operations. Change the data type to a type that has the necessary operations.

Discussion

Developers may choose to use a data type that is less than ideal even when an ideal data type exists. This usually occurs when the programmer is inexperienced and is unaware of the appropriate data type. For example, a programmer may choose to represent a binary value with binary operations as a string because the developer is unfamiliar with bitwise operations. Developers may also choose to use strings because they are easy to read and their operations are familiar. However, using the correct data type is usually more concise [Direct Expression] and more efficient [Computer Science]. Also, trying to figure out how a developer has encoded a mechanism such as bitwise operations into strings is confusing when there exists a more common way to perform the operations [Orthodoxy].

Other examples of inappropriate data types include encoding values into a new format such as integer constants instead of enums, bit fields in integers or delimited strings. While it may be necessary to perform some encoding because of data transfer or storage limitations, be sure the limitations are real and not just an excuse to be clever. You can usually represent encoded fields using a class instead.

Example

The following example uses strings to represent binary values and some convoluted code to perform an exclusive-or. The refactored version of the code uses a more straightforward integer representation. The assumption is that the length of the values does not exceed 32.

Before:

```
String findDisjointBits(String value1,
                               String value2) {

   int minLength = Math.min(value1.length(),
       value2.length());
   String result = "";
   for (int i = 0; i < minLength; i++) {
      if (value1.indexOf(i) == '1') {
         result +=
            value2.indexOf(i) == '1'?'0': '1';
      } else {
         result +=
            value2.indexOf(i) == '0'?'0': '1';
      }
   }

   int maxLength = Math.max(value1.length(),
                      value2.length());
   for (int i = 0; i < maxLength(); i++) {
      result += '0';
   }
   return result;
}
```

After:

```
int findDisjointBits(int value1, int value2) {

   return value1 ^ value2;
}
```

Chapter 6 - Coupling-Based Rules

Coupling deals with the interaction between two modules. Loose coupling, which is to say less interaction, allows the modules to operate more independently – the result is that each module may be considered without concern for the others.

Since principles are ethereal, it is impossible to completely isolate their effects. Therefore, coupling is not the only driving force behind the rules of this section. However, coupling is a major factor in these rules, and these rules help to illustrate the principle of coupling.

Encapsulate Collection

Abstract

A class has a method that returns a field that is a collection. Allow read-only access to the collection and provide methods to operate on the collection.

Discussion

If a class has a method that returns a collection field, the class can no longer keep track and control how other classes may modify the class. For example, a foreign class may request a reference to the collection field, keep the reference and modify the collection at some later and inopportune time. To prevent this, classes should only return read-only access to the collection (preferably via iterators). This may require making a copy of the collection, but this improves the integrity of the class [Coupling].

In addition to only returning read-only references to the collection, the class controlling the collection may want to provide methods to operate on the collection such as add() and remove(). The addition of even more operations may indicate an overlooked abstraction.

Example

In this example, the Organization class has a list of people who are members of the organization. Code using the Organization class may want to review the members of the Organization class. Before the refactoring, the Organization class returns a reference to the list of Person. This can cause a problem, because once external code has a reference to the list, the external code may choose to modify the list at a point when the Organization class least expects it.

Instead, the refactored Organization class provides only an iterator to the list. The iterator assures read-only access to the list so that the code using the iterator will not be able to modify the list. The refactored code goes even further by cloning the list before returning the iterator. Cloning the list is like taking a snapshot of the contents of the list so that if the Organization class decides to modify the list while the accessing code is iterating through the list, there will be no concurrent modification problems. Note that the clone is a shallow clone; in other words, cloning only makes a copy of the list structure and not the Person objects in the list. A shallow copy will prevent concurrent modification problems for the list itself, but not the items in the list. So, for example, changing the name of a Person in the list would affect both the read-only accessing code as well as the Organization's copy.

Before:

```
class Organization {

    ArrayList<Person> members;

    List<Person> getMembers() {
        return members;
    }
    ...
}
```

After:

```
class Organization {

    ArrayList<Person> members;

    Iterator<Person> getMembers() {
        return members.clone.iterator();
    }
    ...
}
```

Encapsulate Field

Abstract

A class has a public field. Make the field private and provide accessor methods.

Discussion

Public fields allow code anywhere to change the internal state of the class. Adding accessor methods provides a level of indirection that hides the actual representation of the field. Quite often the representation is the same as what the accessors expose, but the level of indirection has become a customary mechanism [Orthodoxy] that also allows for the change in representation when necessary [Coupling].

Languages like C# provide convenient syntactic sugar that gives the best of both worlds since fields have an unencumbered interface as if they were public, but there is still a level of indirection that separates the representation from its interface. The important point is not the form of the interface, but the separation of the interface from the representation. In terms of the coupling principle, it makes little difference what the interface looks like as long as it is distinct from the representation so that changing the representation does not affect modules that interact with the field's interface.

This rule illustrates a more general concept, which is the conceptualization of the interface as separate from the design/implementation. The interface establishes a contract between a providing module or service and its consumer. It can be very helpful to compartmentalize the interface separately from the implementation. For example, in a test-driven environment, you can create the necessary tests for a module by merely considering the interface and without looking at the implementation.

Example

This example shows a public name field within a person class. Refactoring makes the field private and provides accessor methods to get and set the value. This is useful for the following scenario. Imagine you have a bug where the name field becomes corrupt at some point. If you have accessor methods in place, you merely need to monitor (perhaps by setting a break point in) the setName method to see who calls the method with the corrupt value. Without the accessor methods, you would need to do a search for all code that changes the value.

Further, imagine you want to store the name field in an encrypted format, but provide access to the field in its unencrypted form. Accessor methods would give you a single place for encrypting and decrypting the field.

Before:

```
class Person {
   public String name;
   ...
}
```

After:

```
class Person {
   private String name;
   public String getName() {
      return name;
   }

   public void setName(String name) {
      this.name = name;
   }
   ...
}
```

Extract Interface

Abstract

Two or more classes have similar behaviors with different implementations. Create an interface for the behaviors.

Discussion

Good design intuition based on principles of coupling [Coupling] will usually uncover interfaces, however, several classes with similar sounding behaviors may indicate that you have overlooked an interface. This is especially true if the behaviors have very different implementations – similar implementations might indicate extracting a superclass instead. Try to create an interface with the common behaviors or a subset of the common behaviors that seem to work together [Cohesion]. Try to give the interface a meaningful name that reflects the group of common behaviors [Metaphor]. If you have difficulty trying to name the interface in a useful way, try different combinations of methods – you may be missing more than one interface. If you can find no useful combination then the interface is likely not useful, so don't create it. However, if you can create the interface, you may benefit by the calling methods being able to use the interface rather than the concrete classes [Limit Interaction].

All things being equal prefer interfaces to inheritance. This is because most of today's languages allow classes to implement many interfaces but only extend one superclass. However, if the behaviors have similar implementations and the relationship between the proposed subclasses and the proposed superclass is an "is-a" relationship, you will want to use inheritance to eliminate redundant code [Normalization].

Example

In this example both the Flintstone class and the Jeston class have draw() methods. However, the implementation of these methods is necessarily different, which means that we don't want to use inheritance. The refactored code shows that both Flintstone and Jetson classes implement the Drawable interface.

Before:

```
class Flintstone {
   void draw() {
   // Draws a stone age cartoon character
   }
}

class Jetson {
   String draw() {
   // Draws a space age cartoon character
   }
}
```

After:

```
interface Drawable {
   void draw();
}

class Flintstone implements Drawable {
   ...
}

class Jetson implements Drawable {
   ...
}
```

Replace Control Parameter

Abstract

A method uses a control parameter to determine behavior. Remove the parameter by splitting the method.

Discussion

When a method relies on a control flag to determine behavior, the calling code usually sets the flag and calls the method. This is, by definition, control coupling. Instead, have the calling code explicitly and directly call a method that performs the function [Coupling, Direct Expression]. Removing the control flag by splitting the method reduces the method's data or message coupling.

Example

Here is an example of a control-coupled math function. The function receives three parameters. The first parameter is the control flag – which means it determines what function the method actually performs (addition, subtraction, multiplication or division). The other two parameters are operands. This example also shows a code snippet that calls the math function.

The refactored code removes the control flag and splits the math method into four separate methods – one for each function. The resulting methods use data coupling, which is preferable to control coupling.

This is clearly a very simple example, but this example illustrates the point quite clearly. Because this example is so simple you may think that nobody would ever do something so awkwardly. However, developers often use control coupling without giving it much thought. For example, imaging a motor control method for a robotics application. The motor controller might need to move the motor forward or backward, so the developer might be tempted to just pass in a control flag to indicate the direction. The motor control example could be further complicated if the motor control method has some prelude or postlude code that is the same independent of the direction of the motor. Developers might argue that control coupling works well because of the common code. However, the common code may be factored into its own methods and called from the two separate methods (i.e., forward() and backward()). This approach eliminates the control coupling while not violating the principle of Normalization.

Before:

```
enum Operation {
    ADD,
    SUBTRACT,
    MULTIPLY,
    DIVIDE
}

void main() {
    float result1 =
    mathFunction(Operation.ADD, 1.0, 1.0);
    print("1.0 + 1.0 = " + result1);

    float result2 =
    mathFunction(Operation.SUBTRACT, 1.0, 1.0);
    print("1.0 - 1.0 = " + result2);

    float result3 =
    mathFunction(Operation.MULTIPLY, 1.0, 1.0);
    print("1.0 * 1.0 = " + result3);

    float result4 =
    mathFunction(Operation.DIVIDE, 1.0, 1.0);
    print("1.0 / 1.0 = " + result4);
```

```
}

float mathFunction(Operation operation,
        float operand1, float operand2) {

   float result;
   switch (operation) {
   case Operation.ADD:
      result = operand1 + operand2;
      break;
   case Operation.SUBTRACT:
      result = operand1 - operand2;
      break;
   case Operation.MULTIPLY:
      result = operand1 * operand2;
      break;
   case Operation.DIVIDE:
      result = operand1 / operand2;
      break;
   }
   return result;
}
```

After:

```
void main() {
   float result1 = add(1.0, 1.0);
   print("1.0 + 1.0 = " + result1);

   float result2 =
   subtract(1.0, 1.0);
   print("1.0 - 1.0 = " + result2);

   float result3 =
   multiply(1.0, 1.0);
   print("1.0 * 1.0 = " + result3);

   float result4 =
   divide(1.0, 1.0);
   print("1.0 / 1.0 = " + result4);
}

float add(float operand1, float operand2) {
   return operand1 + operand2;
}

float subtract(float operand1, float operand2)
{
   return operand1 - operand2;
}

float multiply(float operand1, float operand2)
{
   return operand1 * operand2;
}

float divide(float operand1, float operand2) {
   return operand1 / operand2;
}
```

Replace Stamp Coupling

Abstract

A method receives an object as a parameter, but uses only a small portion of the object's information. Change the parameters of the method to use only the necessary values.

Discussion

A method may need a couple parameter values to perform its task. Sometimes these parameters may reside with in a single larger object. It is tempting just to pass the larger object in since it requires a little less typing. However, this has two undesirable side effects. First, not passing in the precise information necessary for the function can obscure the purpose of the function [Direct Expression]. For example, imagine a function that adds two numbers but is passed an object containing all the information explaining the national economic status and an object that explains the US tax code. On observing the method signature, one would wonder why the method needed all the additional (unused) information. Second, if any of the other fields of the object become inadvertently corrupt, the debugging process must consider all unrelated methods that have access to these fields. Keep methods robust by passing in only the necessary information [Limit Interaction, Coupling].

Example

This example shows a method signature for the method checkTirePressure(). Initially this method receives a Car object. The Car object obviously has the tires, but also include the body, the drivetrain and sundry other information. Clearly the method does not require the entire car to check the tire pressure. The refactored method signature shows that the method only really requires a set of Tire objects.

Before:

```
void checkTirePressure(Car car);
```

After:

```
void checkTirePressure(Set<Tire> tires);
```

Use Interfaces for Collections

Abstract

Collections have interfaces as well as concrete implementations. Use the concrete type when creating a collection, but thereafter refer to the collection using its interface.

Discussion

Each concrete collection has an interface that is a contract for the types of operations the collection provides. For example, sets provide unordered access to their members whereas lists provide ordered access. The different concrete implementations of these collections have different performance characteristics that a developer may choose based on foreknowledge of how the collection is likely to be used. However, since all operations of a collection interface type are the same for all concrete collections, the difference between using two different concrete types occurs only when constructing the concrete type. All other operations are the same.

By referring to a collection by its interface, code that uses the collection can limit referencing the concrete type to its creation. By limiting referencing the concrete type to its creation, if it becomes necessary to change the concrete type, only the line of code that creates the type needs to be changed [Coupling, Limit Interaction].

Example

In the following example, the Cartoon class has a method that reviews a list of characters. The method listCharacters() receives an ArrayList of Character as a parameter and then iterates through the list to perform an operation on each of the characters. However, listCharacters() really doesn't care that the parameter is an ArrayList. All listCharacters() wants to do is iterate through the characters. The listCharacters() method can do this just as easily with a List as with an ArrayList,- making the method more general by using the interface instead of the concrete type.

The refactored version of the Cartoon class changes the parameter type to the List interface. This allows code that uses other forms of lists, such as ArrayList, LinkedList, Stack and Vector, to also use the listCharacters method.

Before:

```
class Cartoon {

    void listCharacters(
            ArrayList<Character> characters) {

        for (Character character : characters) {
            ...
        }
    }
    ...
}
```

After:

```
class Cartoon {

    void listCharacters(List<Character>
characters) {

        for (Character character : characters) {
            ...
        }
    }
    ...
}
```

Chapter 7 - Direct Expression-Based Rules

Computer Science is about conceptualizing systems and communicating those conceptualizations. In other words, Computer Science requires both deep thought and the ability to articulate that thought. One mechanism of articulation is through code.

There is interplay between thought and articulation. Sometimes when we try to articulate our thinking, the communication is not clear. As we work to make our communication more clear we realize that our thinking may not have been thorough. So in order to clearly communicate, we need to stop and think more clearly.

From time to time, software developers may try to communicate an algorithm in code that is not well thought out. The result is code that is convoluted in some manner. Direct expression is about thinking about what you are trying to communicate until your communication is as clear and straightforward as possible. The rules in this chapter illustrate ways to make the communication, via code, clearer and more direct.

Assign Boolean Values Directly

Abstract

Code tests a conditional with an if/then/else and sets a Boolean. Instead, set the value directly from the result of the conditional.

Discussion

If you have code that does a test only to set a Boolean value, replace the entire test with a Boolean assignment [Direct Expression]. Note that you can also use the complement of the test.

In the case where the conditional is a compound conditional, first refactor the compound conditional into a single predicate, and then perform the assignment. In this case you may determine that you may not even need the assignment, as the predicate may be a substitute for the target of the assignment.

Example 1

This example shows a code fragment that checks an age to determine if the individual is young. If the age is less than 18 the code determines that the individual is young, otherwise the code determines the individual is not young. The refactored code expresses this more concisely.

Before:

```
if (age < 18) {
   isYoung = true;
} else {
   isYoung = false;
}
```

After:

```
isYoung = (age < 18);
```

Example 2

Here is a second example that shows how the predicate may eliminate the need for the assignment.

Before:

```
boolean isYoungAndRich;
if ((age < 18) && (salary > 1000000)) {
   isYoungAndRich = true;
} else {
   isYoungAndRich = false;
}
Decimal cost = calculateCost(isYoungAndRich);
```

After:

```
static final int YOUNG_MAX_AGE = 18;
static final int
     RICH_SALARY_THRESHOLD = 1000000;

boolean isYoungAndRich(age,salary) {
   return (age < YOUNG_MAX_AGE) &&
        (salary > RICH_SALARY_THRESHOLD);
}

...
Decimal cost =
   calculateCost(isYoungAndRich(age, salary));
...
```

Eliminate Complements from if-then-else Statements

Abstract

Code has a complemented conditional in an if-then-else. Remove the complement and exchange the then and else clauses.

Discussion

When an if-then-else has a condition that is complemented (i.e., has a "not" in front of it), you can express the same idea by removing the complement and making the then clause the else clause, and the original else clause the then clause. This removes the complement that only complicates the conditional [Direct Expression]. Notice that this only works if there is an else clause.

Often developers will resist this rule because they believe the complemented clause deserves initial attention. While this may be the case on rare occasions, more often than not the developer has not fully conceptualized the problem and is just resisting based on an initial reaction. Conditional expressions are a major source of defects; therefore, anything developers can do to reduce the complexity of conditionals serves to improve the quality of the code.

Example

This example shows code for dealing with the end of a file. If the algorithm reaches the end of the file, it must notify the user. However, if the algorithm has not reached the end of the file, it must continue to read. The pre-refactored code initially deals with what happens under the condition of not reaching the end of file and then handles the case of the end of file.

This adds an unnecessary complement to the conditional.
The refactored code removes this complement.

Before:

```
if (!endOfFile) {
   readMoreStuff();
} else {
   notifyUserOfEndOfFile();
}
```

After:

```
if (endOfFile) {
   notifyUserOfEndOfFile();
} else {
   readMoreStuff();
}
```

Introduce Assertion

Abstract

Code assumes something about the state of the program.
Make assumptions explicit and computationally tractable with
assertions.

Discussion

When developing code the developer may realize that some
condition must exist in the code at some given point. For
example, in order for a method to function properly, the
method assumes that the parameter values are not null.
These assumptions often correspond to preconditions,
invariants or post-conditions. Help readers of the code realize
these assumptions by making them explicit using assertions
[Direct Expression]. Assertions are like comments. They do
not, and should not, affect the algorithmic execution. But
unlike comments, the program checks that assertions are valid
at runtime. So besides having a human readable quality, they
also have an executable quality. However, beware that
assertions may be compiled out of production code.
Therefore assertions must never perform side effects
necessary for the correct execution of the code.

Example

This example shows a method that has several built-in
assumptions. The pre-refactored code shows one of these
assumptions as comments. The refactored version of the
code shows the assumptions explicitly as assertions.

Before:

```
/*
 * Returns a string that is a percentage of
 * the original.
 * @parm source the original source string
 * @parm percent a number in the range [0..99]
 */
String getPercentageOfString(String source,
                             int percent) {
   int length = source.length();
   int numberOfChars = length * percentage /
                                 100;
   return source.substring(0,numberOfChars);
}
```

After:

```
String getPercentageOfString(String source,
                             int percent) {
   assert(source != null);
   assert((percent >= 0) && (percent < 100));

   int length = source.length();
   int numberOfChars = length * percentage /
                                 100;

   assert((numberOfChars >= 0) &&
       (numberOfChars <= source.length()));

   return source.substring(0,numberOfChars);
}
```

Replace Boolean Constant Comparison

Abstract

Code has conditionals that compare Boolean values to true or false constants. Express this same idea without the constant.

Discussion

Comparing a Boolean value to a constant only adds unnecessary clutter. Any comparison to the constant *true* may remove the comparison. Any comparison to the constant *false* may remove the comparison by taking the complement. These are simple refactoring changes that eliminate redundant or unnecessary code [Limit Interaction] and directly state the purpose of the code [Direct Expression].

Example

This example shows two separate equality conditionals; one compares a Boolean value to the constant *true* and the other compares against the constant *false*. The refactoring simplifies the first comparison by just eliminating the comparison. To understand why, consider both cases; if the Boolean value is true, then the result of the comparison is true, and if the Boolean value is false, the result of the comparison is false. Therefore, the result of the comparison always equals the Boolean value. Similarly, if the predicate compares a Boolean value to false, if the value is false, the comparison yields true, and if the value is true, the comparison yields false. So the comparison of a Boolean value to false always yields the complement of the value.

This example also shows two inequality conditionals. Note that any Boolean comparison that has the form of comparing a Boolean value not equal to a constant may be first refactored by changing the sense of the constant and replacing the inequality with an equality operator. This equality operator may then be replaced by removing the comparison as previously described.

Before:

```
if (dogsAreBarking == true) …
if (birdsAreSinging == false)…
if (beesAreHumming != true)…
if (flowersAreBlooming != false)…
```

After:

```
if (dogsAreBarking) …
if (!birdsAreSinging)…
if (!beesAreHumming)…
if (flowersAreBlooming)…
```

Replace Data Value with Object

Abstract

When a primitive data value needs more functionality or the functionality is becoming messy, acknowledge the missing abstraction by creating a class.

Discussion

Sometimes developers use a primitive data type to represent some entity and add methods to the containing class to manipulate the entity. As these manipulative methods multiply and become more involved, it is likely that the developer has shoehorned a first-class object into a primitive.

A common example of entities coerced into primitives occurs when migrating manual systems into automated ones. Quite often manual systems have file names or other identifiers that have encoded fields. For example, an identifier such as "Oct2012Dept1Anderson" indicates a date, a department and a person who is associated with the entity. Developers will also sometimes encode bit fields as multiple types of data as integers.

When a primitive data type encodes multiple fields, you can create a class that explicitly contains each of the fields [Computer science, Direct expression, Orthodoxy]. Once you introduce the new class, if the legacy system still needs to interface with the encoded primitive type, you can provide a constructor on the new class that accepts the encoded primitive as well as a method to produce an instance of the encoded primitive.

Example

In this example the Person class encodes the area code and the phone number into a single string. Refactoring moves the phone number to a class of its own that the Person class can use. The example also includes a constructor and a toString() method that would allow the PhoneNumber class to continue to work with legacy software if necessary.

Before:

```
class Person {
    ...
    String phoneNumber; // e.g., "303-123-4567"

    String getAreaCode() {
       return phoneNumber.split("-")[0];
    }

    String getNumber() {
       String[] phoneParts =
                  phoneNumber.split("-");
       return phoneParts[1] + "-" +
                  phoneParts[2];
    }
    ...
}
```

After:

```
class Person {
    ...
    PhoneNumber phoneNumber;

    PhoneNumber getPhoneNumber() {
       Return phoneNumber;
    }
}

class PhoneNumber {
```

```
    String areaCode;
    String exchange;
    String extension;

    PhoneNumber(String encodedNumber) {
        String[] phoneParts =
                phoneNumber.split("-");
        this(phoneParts[0],phoneParts[1],
                        phoneParts[2]);
    }

    PhoneNumber(String areaCode,
        String exchange, String extension) {
        this.areaCode = areaCode;
        this.exchange = exchange;
        this.extension = extension;
}

    String toString() {
        return areaCode +"-"+ exchange +"-"+
                    extension;
    }

    String getAreaCode() {
        return areaCode
    }

    String getNumber() {
        return exchange + "-" + extension;
    }
}
```

Replace Parallel Arrays with an Object Array

Abstract

Code may use multiple arrays, which associate values between the arrays by using the index. Consolidate the arrays into one array of objects where the fields in the object indicate the meaning instead of the array name.

Discussion

Sometimes as developers write code they choose an array for a collection of primitive values. Then when they need additional related values, they create additional parallel arrays. There is an implicit link between these arrays formed by the array index. Replace this implicit relationship with a more explicit relationship [Direct Expression] by using a single array with fields for the primitives. The direct relationship is not only more expressive, but using one array instead of two reduces the opportunity to inject bugs by letting the two arrays get out of sync. For example, as the arrays grow it becomes possible that modifications to the arrays will result in the orders of the arrays becoming mismatched.

Example

Here is an example of code that has two arrays; one array contains the name of a person. The second array contains the age of the person whose name has the same index value. The refactored result contains only one array, but each element is an object that contains both values.

Before:

```
String[] names = {
   Fred,
   Barney,
   Wilma,
   Betty
};

int[] age = {
   35,
   36,
   27,
   28
};
```

After:

```
class FlintstoneCharacter {
    String name;
    int age;

    FlintstoneCharacter(String name, int age) {
        this.name = name;
        this.age = age;
    }

    String getName() {
        return name;
    }

    String getAge() {
        return age;
    }
}

FlintstoneCharacter[] = {
    new FlintsoneCharacter("Fred", 35),
    new FlintsoneCharacter("Barney", 36),
    new FlintsoneCharacter("Wilma", 27),
    new FlintsoneCharacter("Betty", 28)
};
```

Replace Symbolic Constants with Enum

Abstract

Related symbolic constants often indicate a new type.
Replace all of the related symbolic constants with an enum.

Discussion

While symbolic constants are better than magic numbers, if the symbolic constants are related, they may constitute a new type - i.e., where instances should only have discrete values. By turning these symbolic types into an enum, the relationship between the constants becomes explicit to the point where the compiler can even do type checking [Metaphor, Direct Expression].

Example

In this example, the pre-refactored code uses symbolic constants to map mnemonics to values. Each of the symbolic constants refers to a different blood type. The developer of this code even realized this relationship and tried to represent the relationship with the same prefix for each symbolic constant (i.e., "BLOOD_TYPE").

Although the prefix of the symbolic constant is helpful to the human reader, the prefix is not computationally tractable – the computer can't make sense of the relationship based on the prefix. For example, imagine a method that receives a blood type as a parameter. The logical type of the parameter is "blood type", but the computational type of the parameter is integer. Therefore, calling code could legally pass any integer to the method, even those that do not represent a blood type.

Converting the computational type to match the logical type (i.e., making the integer be blood type) allows the compiler to do type checking for us to make sure we are actually passing in a blood type. The refactored code shows what this would look like.

Before:

```
...
public static final int BLOOD_TYPE_O = 0;
public static final int BLOOD_TYPE_A = 1;
public static final int BLOOD_TYPE_B = 2;
public static final int BLOOD_TYPE_AB = 3;
...
void performTransfusion(int bloodType) {
    ...
}
```

After:

```
public enum BloodType {
    O,
    A,
    B,
    AB
}

void performTransfusion(BloodType bloodType) {
    ...
}
```

Reserve Inheritance for "is-a" Relationships

Abstract

A set of classes uses inheritance to represent a relationship, which is not truly an "is-a" type of relationship. Refactor the functionality of the classes to eliminate the inheritance.

Discussion

Inheritance should only be used to represent "is-a" relationships. Using inheritance for other purposes can be confusing because developers expect inheritance to represent "is-a" relationships [Orthodoxy, Direct Expression]. A generally acceptable design philosophy is that classes should be open for extension but closed for modification. When designers follow this philosophy, they can extend the functionality of classes without having to change the class itself. This is great because it means that developers can create and test classes that others can use with confidence, knowing the class is solid. However, if designers do not follow this open/closed philosophy, the resulting classes become difficult to extend without changing them.

When faced with non-extensible classes, developers may be tempted to use inheritance to add functionality. Using inheritance to merely extend a class' functionality when the extension does not represent an "is-a" relationship sends a mixed semantic design message to those trying to understand the classes' relationships. On the one hand the relationship appears to be an explicit "is-a" relationship. On the other hand, it seems that the derived class really doesn't have the inheritance relationship. Therefore, those trying to understand the design and relationships are left to wonder where the dissonance lies. Does the person misunderstand the design, or is the design poorly formed?

If the original design of the base class does not support the open/close philosophy, it may be necessary to open the class for modification and make the class extensible. Sometimes this may not be possible because, for example, the original source is not available. In this case, rather than extend the class with inheritance and create the semantic dissonance, you may be able to create a wrapper class that is open for extension but closed for modification. This solution will not work well if there are many other closed classes that use the original base class as you would need to extend each of these additional classes. In this case you could create a separate static helper class that would provide the additional functionality, but does not abuse the inheritance relationship.

Example 1

In this example, the original Person class has a birthdate. The extending class adds a method to get the age – a nice feature that would have been nice in the original Person class. However, the notion of the class PersonWithAge is bogus. The Person class should really contain this method.

Before:

```
class Person {

   void setBirthdate(Date birthdate) {
      ...
   }

   Date getBirthdate() {
      ...
   }
}

class PersonWithAge() extends Person {

   int getAge() {
      ...
   }
}
```

After:

```
class Person {

   void setBirthdate(Date birthdate) {
      ...
   }

   Date getBirthdate() {
      ...
   }

   int getAge() {
      ...
   }
}
```

Example 2

Here is an example similar to the previous one, except that the
Person class is completely closed and other classes use the
Person class. The solution is to add a static helper class.

Before:

```
class Person {
   void setBirthdate(Date birthdate);
   // Implementation is closed

   Date getBirthdate();
   // Implementation is closed
}

class PersonWithAge() extends Person {

   int getAge() {
      ...
   }
}
```

After:

```
class Person {

   void setBirthdate(Date birthdate);
   // Implementation is closed

   Date getBirthdate();
   // Implementation is closed
}

static class AgeHelper() {

   static int getAge(Person person) {
      ...
   }
}
```

Use Ternaries for if-then-else Assignments

Abstract

Both the *then* and *else* clauses only assign a value to the same variable. Use a ternary to express this idea.

Discussion

When code has a conditional that determines which value to assign to a variable, a ternary expresses this concept more directly [Direct Expression]. A ternary makes it very clear that the purpose of the statement is to assign a value, whereas, an if/then/else statement obfuscates this fact.

In the case where code uses a conditional to determine which values to assign to several variables, it is best not to use the ternary form. Using a ternary form across several assignments would require duplication of the conditional, which would violate the Normalization Principle.

Example

Here is a simple example that illustrates the point of this rule. In the pre-refactored code you notice that you have to consider a few different things before you get the gist of the code. For most people, the code first draws your eyes to the conditional. Once you understand the conditional you inspect the *then* clause. Finally, you notice the *else* clause. You realize that there is something familiar about the *else* clause so you naturally compare *else* clause back to the *then* clause and realize they both assign a value to the same variable. At this point you grasp that the purpose of this entire section of code is just to assign a value to a variable.

In the refactored code, the first thing you realize is that the code is performing an assignment. You then notice the form of the ternary and inspect the conditional. Finally, you look to see what the two possible values are. This seems to require less cognitive load.

Before:

```
if (yourDogBites) {
   numberOfTreats = 0;
} else {
   numberOfTreats = 3;
}
```

After:

```
numberOfTreats = (yourDogBites)? 0: 3;
```

Chapter 8 - Limit Interaction-Based Rules

Limit interaction is closely related to coupling, but is distinct enough that it warrants its own principle. Perhaps the most colloquial definition of limit interaction might be stated as, "avoid clutter". In other words, constrain the effects of unrelated data and behaviors.

Think about clutter. The problem with clutter is not necessarily that the objects cluttering some area are not helpful or useful; the problem has to do more with their organization and overall influence on the cluttered area. Another aspect of clutter is that clutter does not usually arise from a single majorly misplaced item, but from many minor misplacements that snowball into an overwhelming feeling of unease.

Perhaps you have had the experience of trying to work in a cluttered area and have found it unsettling. Similarly in software, clutter can be annoying. Clutter has no single cause, but arises from inattention to detail. Some people allow clutter to build up and then require a significant investment to clean up the clutter. A more scalable approach is to deal with the details as they arise – avoiding the *spring-cleaning* affect.

The rules in this chapter should help developers avoid clutter in their code.

Introduce Null Object

Abstract

Code repeatedly checks for null values. Replace the null
value with a null object.

Discussion

According to Martin Fowler, the essence of polymorphism is
that instead of asking each object what type of object it is and
invoking some behavior, just invoke the behavior and let the
object know what that means. Code often uses null values as
a checkable value. If the value is null, then the code behaves
in a special manner. This is contrary to polymorphism. So
instead of checking for null values, create a null object with
null behaviors [Limit Interaction].

Example

Here is an example of a ringtone manager. The manager
allows the user to select one of several ringtones or to select
no ringtone. In the pre-refactored code, the ringtone manager
must check for the special case of no ringtone and behave
accordingly. The refactored code introduces a NullRingtone
that makes no sound – effectively a null object. This null
object allows the ringtone manager to use the standard code
paths for all cases.

Before:

```
class RingtoneManager {

   interface Ringtone {
      String getName();
      void play();
   }

   Ringtone[] ringtones;
   Ringtone current = null;
   …

   void setCurrentRingtone(Ringtone current) {
      this.current = current;
   }

   void displayRingtones() {
      display("No Ringtone");
      for (Ringtone tone : ringtones) {
         display(tone.getName());
      }
      if (current == null) {
         display("Current tone is no tone");
      } else {
         display("Current tone is "+
                      current.getName());
      }
   }

   void playCurrentRingtone() {
      if (current != null) {
         current.play();
      }
   }
}
```

After:

```
class RingtoneManager {

  interface Ringtone {
    String getName();
    void play();
  }

  class NoRingtone implements Ringtone {
    String getName() {
      Return "No tone";
    }
    void play() {
    }
  }

  Ringtone[] ringtones;
  Ringtone current = null;
  ...

  void setCurrentRingtone(Ringtone current) {
    this.current = current;
  }

  void displayRingtones() {
    for (Ringtone tone : ringtones) {
      display(tone.getName());
    }
    display("Current tone is "+
                current.getName());
  }

  void playCurrentRingtone() {
    current.play();
  }
}
```

Limit Variable Scope

Abstract

Code declares a variable with scope broader than necessary for its use. Move the variable declaration so as to limit its scope as much as possible.

Discussion

Some programmers like to declare all variables at the top of the methods, or even worse, declare class-level fields that could be local variables. By moving variable declarations to limit their scope as much as possible you don't have to worry about extraneous modifications to the variable [Limit Interaction]. Also, the fewer number of variables developers need to consider at any given point in code, the lower the conceptual load on the developer. Lower conceptual load results in developers being able to develop more quickly and with fewer defects.

Sometimes, to understand the effects of an approach, try considering the extreme cases. In this case, consider the problems that could occur if all variables had a global scope. It would be very difficult to determine which sections of code needed which variables. You could imagine developers getting confused and assigning values to the wrong variables. It might even become difficult to assign names to the variables so that the names did not conflict.

All of the problems that could occur if all variables were global, are essentially the same problems, to a lesser extent, developers experience when they allow variable declarations to reach beyond the variables' usefulness. Since every variable has a relationship to every other variable, there is a geometric growth in the relationships between variables. So as the number of variables grows, the number of relationships becomes astronomical. Therefore it is important to limit the number of variables within a section of code as much as possible. This, however, does not imply reusing variables for multiple distinct uses, but instead implies declaring variables with the least possible scope.

Another extreme would be to limit the scope by trying to eliminate the variable completely. For example, code that takes the result of one expression and, instead of storing it in a variable, uses the result in another expression, would not have to declare a variable at all. However, this is not really helpful. Although the variable never exists in code, the variable still exists conceptually – or in other words, just because you don't store the result of an expression in a variable doesn't mean the variable logically ceases to exist. The variable still logically exists, but there is no articulation to help the reader of the code understand what the result of the expression is. At this point limiting interaction starts to impinge on metaphor. So while chaining expressions together may eliminate variables in the code, this practice actually can increase conceptual load. Therefore, developers should avoid this practice for the purpose of limiting scope.

Example

Usually we think of limiting scope to mean declaring variables in the method or block where the code uses them. While limiting the variable scope to the correct code block is helpful, Developers can limit scope even further by postponing variable declarations until the code uses the variable.

This example shows a method that uses three variables and declares them at the beginning of the method. The refactored code declares the variables as the method uses them.

Before:

```
void checkBloodPressure(int lowerBound,
                        int upperBound) {

    int reading;
    int normalizedValue;
    Boolean alertRequired = false;

    reading = readBllodPressure();
    normalizedValue = normalizeReading();
    alertRequired =
        (normalizedValue < lowerBound) ||
        (normalizedValue > upperBound);

    ...

}
```

After:

```
void checkBloodPressure(int lowerBound,
                        int upperBound) {

    int reading = readBloodPressure();
    int normalizedValue = normalizeReading();
    Boolean alertRequired =
            (normalizedValue < lowerBound) ||
            (normalizedValue > upperBound);

    ...

}
```

Maintain Consistent Conceptual Level for Loop

Abstract

An algorithm containing a loop hides part of the looping construct. Expose the loops precondition, invariant and post-condition within the same method.

Discussion

Developers can think about any loop as having a precondition, an invariant and a post condition. In a standard *for* loop the precondition is the initial value of the looping variable; the invariant is that the looping variable is less than the boundary value of the loop; and the post-condition is that the looping variable is greater than or equal to the boundary value.

Sometimes developers will bury one of these parts of the loop in a method so that it becomes difficult to understand the loop by looking at a single method. In these cases it is important to refactor the code so that the method that contains the loop presents all three aspects. Notice that when all three aspects of the loop occur in the same method, the method explains the entire loop [Cohesion] and is less reliant on other methods [Coupling], as the looping related data is not scattered across several methods [Limit Interaction]. In addition, the loop is much easier for people to understand because they can easily find the familiar aspects of the loop [Orthodoxy].

Example

In this example, the code misuses a class' field as the looping variable. Notice that the static initializer sets the precondition by initializing the looping variable; the test for the exit condition takes place in the method containing the loop, and a separate method increments the looping variable.

The refactored code moves all three of these aspects of the loop into the same method.

Before:

```
class Dog {

    int numberOfBarks = 0;
    static final int MAX_BARKS = 10;

    void annoyNeighbors() {

        while (numberOfBarks < MAX_BARKS) {
            ...
            jumpOnFence();
            bark();
            ...
        }
        numberOfBarks = 0;
    }

    void jumpOnFence() {
        ...
    }

    void bark() {
        // Play barking sound
        numberOfBarks++;
    }
}
```

After:

```
class Dog {

    static final int MAX_BARKS = 10;

    void annoyNeighbors() {
        for (int i = 0; (i < MAX_BARKS); i++) {
            ...
            jumpOnFence();
            bark();
            ...
        }
    }

    void jumpOnFence() {
        ...
    }

    void bark() {
        // Play barking sound
    }
}
```

Prefer Variables to Fields

Abstract

If a method uses field values that are not central to the class' abstraction, replace the fields with variables and parameters.

Discussion

Programmers sometimes use fields to hold values that a method within the class uses. Also, developers may use fields to communicate information between methods. In both of these cases the field values really are only useful to the methods and don't support the abstraction of the class. Eliminate these fields and use variables and parameters instead [Cohesion]. Using variables and parameters not only strengthens the cohesion of the class, but the parameters also make the function of the method more explicit [Direct Expression]. Also, using variables and parameters limits the scope of the values [Limit Interaction].

Beware that the number of methods using a value does not indicate that a value should or should not be a field. For example, classes may have legitimate fields that only one method uses, or alternatively a class may have dubious fields that many methods of the class use. The choice of what is a field and what is a variable depends on the class' abstraction and not how many methods use the field. If the value is an integral part of the state of the class, the value should be a field. If the value is not part of the state of the class, the value should be a variable or parameter. While the number of methods that use a value has a high correlation to the legitimacy of a value being a field, it is not a perfect correlation.

Example

Here is an example of a stack class that has a getNthValue()
method. This method returns the nth value from the top of the
stack. Notice that the method receives no parameters and
must determine N from a field value.

In this example, N is not an integral part of the stack
abstraction and is more like tramp data the stack maintains.
The refactored code makes the value a parameter to the
method.

Before:

```
class Stack {

    Object[] objects;
    int nth;

    ...

    void setNth(int nth) {
        this.nth = nth;
    }

    Object getNthValue() {
        Return objects[nth];
    }

    ...

}
```

After:

```
class Stack {

   Object[] objects;

   ...

   Object getNthValue(int nth) {
      Return objects[nth];
   }

   ...

}
```

Replace Inheritance with Delegation

Abstract

An inheritance hierarchy has been normalized to the point that there are many confusing levels. Consider replacing inheritance with delegation.

Discussion

Sometimes as we work to normalize inheritance hierarchies, they become cumbersome and confusing – it becomes hard to determine where implementations of certain functionality occur. One of the reasons for creating Object Oriented Programming and abstraction is to limit the number of interactions we need to consider within an abstraction. Deep and complex inheritance hierarchies effectively eliminate the benefits of abstraction since determining the behavior requires considering nearly the entire hierarchy. In these situations it may be helpful to use delegation in place of inheritance. Delegation allows developers to draw from a set of behaviors to create functionality and effectively flatten the hierarchy [Limit Interaction].

Example

This example shows a complex class hierarchy related to car engines. Each engine requires a starting procedure, but the procedure varies depending on characteristics of the engine. In order to provide the necessary starting procedures, the hierarchy must represent all combinations of features (this example only shows a subset of the combinations, but hopefully enough of a subset to give the general idea).

The refactored code flattens the hierarchy and provides a startMethod delegate. The constructors in the refactored code assign the required start method to the delegate. The delegate eliminates the need for a deep inheritance hierarchy, which makes it much easier to understand.

Before:

```
class CarEngine {
   void start() {
   // Standard starting mechanism
   }
   ...
}

class HighTorqueEngine extends CarEngine {
   void start() {
   // Higher torque starting mechanism
   }
   ...
}

class LowTorqueEngine extends CarEngine {
   void start() {
   // Lower torque starting mechanism
   }
   ...
}

class MonoValveEngine extends
               HighTorqueEngine {
   void start() {
   // Slow starting mechanism
   }
   ...
}

class TwinValveEngine extends
               HighTorqueEngine {
   void start() {
   // Fast starting mechanism
   }
   ...
```

```
}

class V8MonoEngine extends MonoValveEngine {
   ...
}

class V8TwinEngine extends TwinValveEngine {
   void start() {
   // Short starting mechanism
   }
   ...
}
...
```

After:

```
class CarEngine {

   StartMethod startMethod = standardStart;

   void start() {
      this.startMethod();
   }

   void standardStart() {
      // Standard starting mechanism
   }

   void fastStart() {
      // Fast starting mechanism
   }

   void slowStart() {
      // Slow starting mechanism
   }

   void shortStart() {
      // Short starting mechanism
   }
```

```java
    void highTorqueStart() {
        // High torque starting mechanism
    }

    void lowTorqueStart() {
        // Low Torque starting mechanism
    }
    ...
}

class V8MonoEngine extends CarEngine {

    V8MonoEngine() {
        startMethod = slowStart;
    }
    ...
}

class V8TwinEngine extends CarEngine {

    V8TwinEngine() {
        startMethod = shortStart;
    }
    ...
}
```

Chapter 9 - Metaphor-Based Rules

One way to understand an unfamiliar and complex system is to relate the unfamiliar system to a known system. This is the notion of Metaphor.

One of the most useful mechanisms for employing the principle of metaphor is naming. The names we choose for variables, methods and classes, etc. indicate a metaphor. When we name a class Dog, we aren't actually saying the class is a dog, but we are saying the class has characteristics similar to those of a dog.

Metaphors are powerful tools to help developers quickly and implicitly understand complex systems and their relationships – a way to leverage the things a person has already learned.

Introduce Explaining Variable

Abstract

Store the results of an expression in a variable that explains what the expression is.

Discussion

Software sometimes requires a developer to create a complicated expression. As the developer creates the expression, it may be apparent to the developer what the expression means because the developer is deeply steeped in the thought that produced the expression. However, developers who are not in the same mindset may find it difficult to understand the expression.

Sometimes developers recognize that it may be difficult to decipher the expression so they may try to explain the expression with comments. The issue with comments is that the comments can become out of date. The only thing worse than no comments to help you understand an expression is incorrect comments that misrepresent an expression. Since comments inevitably will become out of date, the best state to seek is one with no comments, but with code that is self-documenting.

In order to help developers understand the initial mindset that created an expression, use variables to represent intermediate values within the expression [Metaphor].

Some developers may complain that adding an explaining variable takes up more memory and slows execution. This complaint is generally unfounded since most compilers will optimize the final executable code so that there is no actual difference between source with or without the temporary variable. So, temporary variables serve as human readable and computationally tractable conveniences. These variables also make it much more convenient when debugging a complex expression.

Example

This example shows a method to calculate the difference between the sum of the squares and the square of the sums. The refactored code employs intermediate variables.

Before:

```
int sumOfSquaresMinusSquareOfSum(int[] values)
{
   int result = 0;
   int sum = 0;
   for (int n : values) {
      result += n * n;
      sum += n;
   }
   return result - (sum * sum);
}
```

After:

```
int sumOfSquaresMinusSquareOfSum(int[] values)
{
   int sumOfSquares = 0;
   int sum = 0;
   for (int n : values) {
      sumOfSquares += n * n;
      sum += n;
   }
   int squareOfSum = sum * sum;
   return sumOfSquares - squareOfSum;
}
```

Focus Variable Usage

Abstract

When code uses a variable for more than one reason, separate the uses into different variables, each with its own focus.

Discussion

Software may use the same variable for more than one reason. This can be confusing because the name of the variable can only reflect a single purpose (more often the variable name is something like "temp" that has no reflection of the variable's purpose). So using a variable for more than one purpose is a violation of the principle of metaphor.

A possible indication of this problem is a variable that has more than one assignment. This is not conclusive since some variables may be accumulators. Accumulators may have multiple assignments, such as in a loop, but these variables still only serve a single purpose. To help indicate accumulators, code may use the form of += or *= types of operator/assignments.

Instead of using a single variable for multiple uses, introduce an additional variable for each unique purpose [Cohesion] and name the variables accordingly [Metaphor]. While some may complain that the additional variables add overhead due to additional memory usage, most modern compilers will optimize these variables into registers and reuse the registers so that the variables become a code convenience. Further, if one is concerned about using too much memory, perhaps there is a way to limit the scope of each of the purposes of the variable [Limit Interaction] thereby improving the design quality of the software.

Example

This example prints out the perimeter and area of a rectangle. The first version of the refactored code replaces the multi-purposed *temp* variable with *perimeter* and *area*. The second version of the refactored code also isolates the variables within methods.

Before:

```
void printRectangleAttributes(int height,
                int width) {
  int temp = (2 * height) + (2 * width);
  print("the perimeter is " + temp);

  temp = height * width;
  print("the area is " + temp);
}
```

After:

```
void printRectangleAttributes(int height,
                int width) {
  int perimeter = (2 * height) + (2 * width);
  print("the perimeter is " + perimeter);

  int area = height * width;
  print("the area is " + area);
}
```

After extracting methods to limit variable scope (note that the extracted methods are cohesive using only data coupling):

```
void printRectangleAttributes(int height,
                 int width) {
   printPerimeter(height, width);
   printArea(height, width);
}

void printPerimeter(int height, int width) {
   int perimeter = (2 * height) + (2 * width);
   print("the perimeter is " + perimeter);
}

void printArea(int height, int width) {
   int area = height * width;
   print("the area is " + area);
}
```

Remove Assignments to Parameters

Abstract

When code assigns values to input parameters, introduce variables to eliminate the changing of input parameters.

Discussion

Sometimes code will use input parameters as variables and change the value of the input parameters. This often happens when a programmer needs to change a method so that the input parameter gets adjusted before performing the remainder of the computation of the method. However, changing input parameter values can be very confusing. Those maintaining the method may inadvertently overlook the changes to the input parameter values [Orthodoxy]. Additionally, if the value of the input parameter changes, then the meaning of the value must have also changed, which requires a renaming of the value [Metaphor]. For these reasons, developers should hold the values of input parameters invariant.

Example

This example draws a scaled box. The pre-refactored code changes the value of the bottom-right point. The refactored code uses an adjusted point instead.

Before:

```
void drawScaledBox(Point topLeft,
              Point bottomRight) {
  int height = topLeft.getY() —
              bottomRight.getY();
  int width = topLeft.getX() —
              bottomRight.getX();
  bottomRight.setY(topLeft.getY() +
              scale(height));
  bottomRight.setX(topLeft.getX +
              scale(width));

  drawLine(topLeft.getX(), topLeft.getY(),
     topLeft.getX(), bottomRight.getY());
  drawLine(topLeft.getX(), topLeft.getY(),
     bottomRight.getX(),topLeft.getY());
  drawLine(topLeft.getX(),bottomRight.getY(),
     bottomRight.getX(), bottomRight.getY());
  drawLine(bottomRight.getX(),topLeft.getY(),
     bottomRight.getX(), bottomRight.getY());
}
```

After:

```
void drawScaledBox(Point topLeft,
                Point bottomRight) {
    int height = topLeft.getY() -
                bottomRight.getY();
    int width = topLeft.getX() -
                bottomRight.getX();
    Point adjustedPoint Point(
        topLeft.getY() + scale(height),
        topLeft.getX + scale(width));

    drawLine(topLeft.getX(), topLeft.getY(),
        topLeft.getX(),adjustedPoint.getY());
    drawLine(topLeft.getX(), topLeft.getY(),
        adjustedPoint.getX(),topLeft.getY());
    drawLine(topLeft.getX(),
                    adjustedPoint.getY(),

    adjustedPoint.getX(),adjustedPoint.getY());
    drawLine(adjustedPoint.getX(),
                    topLeft.getY(),

    adjustedPoint.getX(),adjustedPoint.getY());
}
```

Rename Mnemonic

Abstract

The name of a method, variable, field, class or constant does not explain what it does. Rename the Mnemonic.

Discussion

Many rules for refactoring encourage the creation and extraction of many new methods and variables, etc. If these constructs are not named well, the code can become even more confusing. Therefore, as you read through code and find that a name is misleading or uninformative, rename the construct to something more helpful [Metaphor].

A common problem is that developers select names that have overloaded words. For example, the word *transaction* could mean a database operation, a banking transfer or a transfer of goods and services. Developers can use qualifiers to disambiguate overloaded words, but usually the difficulty stems from not being aware that the word is overloaded in the first place. So even though developers strive to select meaning names in the first place, developers often need to rename variables and parameters as it becomes apparent that the names are confusing.

When naming methods, it is often helpful to use a verb and an object (e.g., throwStone() or printReport()). Quite often, method names are unhelpful because they are not specific enough in the verb or the object (e.g., processStuff()). Try replacing the verb with a more explicit verb and the noun with a more specific noun. You may also use adverbs and adjectives to provide specificity.

Variable names should be noun phrases. Helpful noun phrases might include adjectives. Try to avoid abbreviations, especially abbreviations that might be misinterpreted. For example, a name *trk* might mean track, trunk or truck. A few extra characters will not slow down coding or cause the code to be too bulky, but a few extra characters could save a reader of the code significant frustration resulting from a misunderstanding.

Example

Some developers don't seem to see the poor choice of names as a real concern. This example demonstrates the real affects of poor naming. The following is a full Java program with extremely obfuscated naming. Unlike other examples in this book, this example is not refactored. The proof is left to the reader.

Before:

```
public class _{interface __ {int _(int
_);;}static int ___;static{___++;}public static
void main(String[] _){for(int
__=___;__<___<<(___<<(___<<___)));
__++)System.out.println(new __(){public int
_(int _){int __=___;return _==___?__-
__:_==(__<<__)?__:_(_-__)+_(_-
(__<<___)));}}._(__));}}
```

Replace Array with Object

Abstract

The code has an array in which certain elements mean different things. Replace the array with an object that has a field for each element.

Discussion

Sometimes code uses an array where the position of the value in the array indicates a specific meaning. Arrays should be used to store similar objects such that the position of the element in the array is not semantic [Orthodoxy, Computer Science]. By replacing an array of this type with a class where the fields contain the elements, the field names indicate the meaning of the value [Metaphor].

Example

This example shows the parts of a phone number stored as elements of an array such that element 0 is the area code, element 1 is the exchange and element 2 is the extension. Some developers may try to employ metaphor by using an enum to index the array. However, using a class directly expresses the meaning in an orthodox manner.

Before:

```
enum PhoneIndex {
   AREA_CODE = 0,
   EXCHANGE = 1,
   EXTENSION = 2
};

String[] phoneNumber;
phoneNumber[PhoneIndex.AREA_CODE] = "303";
phoneNumber[PhoneIndex.EXCHANGE] = "123";
phoneNumber[PhoneIndex.EXTENSION] = "4567";
```

After:

```
class PhoneNumber {
   String areaCode;
   String exchange;
   String extension;

   PhoneNumber(String areaCode,
               String exchange,
               String extension) {
     this.areaCode = areaCode;
     this.exchange = exchange;
     this.extension = extension;
   }

   void setAreaCode(String areaCode) {
     this.areaCode = areaCode;
   }

   String getAreaCode() {
     return areaCode
   }

   void setExchange(String exchange) {
     this.exchange = exchange;
   }
```

```
String getExchange() {
   return exchange;
}

void setExtension(String extension) {
   this. extension = extension;
}

String getExtension() {
   return extension
}

}

...
PhoneNumber phoneNumber =
    new PhoneNumber("303", "123", "4567);
```

Replace Compound Conditional with Predicate

Abstract

Code has a conditional with more than one Boolean expression. Replace the Boolean expressions with a single self-documenting method.

Discussion

Conditionals, either in branches or loops, are a major source of errors within programs. Replacing complex conditionals with self-documenting predicates forces you to articulate the conditions. Articulating conditions has several useful side-effects; the conditionals become easier to read and understand [Metaphor], the purpose of the conditionals become extremely clear [Direct Expression] and the resultant clarity makes it easier to test and debug [Limit Interaction]. Even conditionals that have only one comparison may benefit from creating a self-documenting predicate.

Example

Here is a simple example that shows a conditional with two Boolean expressions. The expressions check that a date is after the start of summer and before the end of summer. The combination of these two expressions determines if the date occurs during the summer. Therefore, refactoring replaces the two Boolean expressions with a simple predicate named *isSummer()*.

A side effect of producing these types of predicates is reuse. When developers introduce even simple predicates, they become more aware and disposed to reuse the predicates. The result is that all the code has less redundancy and imposes less cognitive load.

Before:

```
if (date.after(SUMMER_START) &&
          date.before(SUMMER_END))…
```

After:

```
if (isSummer())…

boolean isSummer() {
  return (date.after(SUMMER_START) &&
    date.before(SUMMER_END));
}
```

Replace Magic Value with Symbolic Constant

Abstract

Code may have a literal value with a particular meaning.
Create a constant with a name that reflects its meaning.
Replace the literal with the constant.

Discussion

Literal constants in code can be very confusing because the
literal's semantic context is not always clear. Developers refer
to these literal constants as *magic numbers.* Make the context
clear by creating a named constant [Metaphor]. Note, this rule
may also apply to string literals. Also, make sure the name of
the symbolic constant carries useful meaning. For example,
don't use SEVEN for the literal 7. Instead use something that
indicates the context for how the code uses the literal like
NUMBER_OF_DWARVES.

Example

The following example calculates the number of pences for a
given value. The conversion rate may not be familiar to many,
so the use of the constant values of 20 and 12 may be
confusing.

The refactored code names the symbolic constants and
explains what the constants are.

Before:

```
int calculatePence(int pounds, int shillings,
                   int pence) {
   return (pounds * 20 + shillings) * 12 +
                   pence;
}
```

After:

```
static final int PENCE_PER_SHILLING = 12;
static final int SHILLINGS_PER_POUND = 20;

int calculatePence(int pounds, int shillings,
                   int pence) {
   int totalShillings = pounds *
           SHILLINGS_PER_POUND + shillings;
   int totalPence = totalShillings *
           PENCE_PER_SHILLING + pence;
   return totalPence;
}
```

Chapter 10 - Normalization-Based Rules

Normalization refers to eliminating redundancy. Introductory students of Computer Science learn that they can maintain more easily their software if they move reused sections of code into a method or procedure. The first major benefit is, if the reused sections of code require change, duplicated code requires many changes whereas code that resides in only one place requires only one change.

Besides having to change code, there are a host of additional problems that result from redundancy. For example, redundant data makes it difficult to know which data values to trust when the data values disagree.

Note that redundancy may occur in both data and control aspects of software. The rules in this chapter explain how to eliminate redundancy in both data and control.

Consolidate Conditional Expressions

Abstract

Code has multiple conditions that have the same result.
Combine them into a single conditional.

Discussion

Sometimes when designing code it may be helpful to think
through the various states that may occur and handle each of
them separately. This can lead to code duplication. You can
remove this duplication by consolidating the conditionals into a
single expression with a single resultant action
[Normalization]. Often, performing this consolidation will help
you identify and articulate a compound conditional that is a
result of all the sub-conditionals. In these cases you can
create a predicate to encapsulate the conditionals and
document the compound conditional [Metaphor].

It is reasonable to choose not to apply this rule if it is very
clear that the conditionals will need to be separated in the
near future in order to add functionality.

Example

This example shows three if/else branches that all perform the
same calculation (i.e., setting amount to zero). To refactor this
code, we would first combine all the conditionals using logical
or operators. However, once we combine the conditionals, it
becomes clearer to us that these conditions really constitute a
compound conditional that determines eligibility for disability,
so we also refactor by extracting a self-documenting
predicate.

Before:

```
if (seniority < 2) {
   amount = 0;
} else if (monthsDisabled >= 12) {
   amount = 0;
} else if (isPartTime) {
   amount = 0;
}
```

After:

```
if (!isEligibleForDisability()) {
   amount = 0;
}

static final int MIN_YEARS_SENIORITY = 2;
static final int MAX_MONTHS_OF_DISABILITY =
                                        12;

boolean isEligibleForDisability() {
   return (seniority >= MIN_YEARS_SENIORITY)&&
      (monthsDisabled <
            MAX_MONTHS_OF_DISABILITY)&&
      !isPartTime;
}
```

Consolidate Duplicate Fragments

Abstract

The same fragment of code exists in all conditions. Move the fragment outside of the conditional.

Discussion

When you notice that both the *then* and the *else* clauses have the same fragment of code, you can move the code fragment outside of the conditional. This eliminates redundancy [Normalization] and also makes it clearer what the conditional affects [Direct Expression].

When conditional clauses need refactoring in this way, part of the clauses are the same and part of the clauses differ. The portion of the clauses that differs is the *variant sub-clause*. If there is a portion of the clause before the variant sub-clause, that invariant portion may be moved to before the conditional. Likewise, if there is a portion of the clause after the variant sub-clause, that invariant portion may be moved after the conditional.

Example

This example has a conditional that determines if the dog bites. If the dog bites, the example wants to call the dog, kick the dog and feed the dog. If the dog does not bite, the example wants to call the dog, pet the dog and feed the dog. In this example, the variant sub clause is the section where the example either kicks or pets the dog. Therefore, the refactored code can move calling the dog to before the conditional and feeding the dog to after the conditional. In other words, we want to call the dog and feed the dog whether or not the dog bites. We only need to know if the dog bites to determine if we should kick the dog or pet the dog. The refactored code makes this distinction.

Before:

```
if (yourDogBites()) {
   callTheDog();
   kickTheDog();
   feedTheDog();
} else {
   callTheDog();
   petTheDog();
   feedTheDog();
}
```

After:

```
callTheDog();

if (yourDogBites()) {
   kickTheDog();
} else {
   petTheDog();
}

feedTheDog();
```

Extract Method

Abstract

Convert a code fragment into a method.

Discussion

Most developers think of using methods to abstract code so that the code can be reused in multiple places [Normalization]. While this is certainly an important reason for creating a method, it is not the only justification.

Computation comes in many forms. Examples include machine language instructions, high-level language statements, code blocks, loops, methods and processes. Each of these computations is similar in that each has inputs and outputs, preconditions, post-conditions and invariants. So by extracting a method, you create a formal computational abstraction.

These method abstractions allow you to name them in a way that suggests the function of the computation [Metaphor]. Naming methods with functional names allows the code that calls the method to be more concise [Direct Expression]. In addition, the method can hide complicating details from the calling code [Limit Interaction].

A common indication of the need for method extraction includes duplicated or near duplicated code. In this case the method extraction eliminates the duplicate code [Normalization]. Another indicator for method extraction is a method with many (i.e., more than about seven) lines of code. Similarly, long or complex code may have comments explaining what it is doing. When a method is long or complicated, extracting methods can make the method more digestible and self-documenting [Limit Interaction, Direct Expression].

Care should be taken to extract methods based on computational functionality [Cohesion] and not just lines of code or code commonality. Often reoccurring lines of code can be a good indicator that you need to extract a method, but seeing reoccurring lines should not be the only concern when abstracting a method. Also, since the computational functionality is significant, it is sometimes desirable to extract a method even if the resulting method has only one line of code.

Example 1

This first example shows duplicate code. The refactored code extracts these lines into a method. Notice that these lines correspond with the notion of caring for the pet. Therefore, extracting the method is reasonable.

Before:

```
void feedAnimal(Animal animal) {
    if (animal.isHungry()) {
        Food food = obtainFood();
        food.prepare();
        animal.feed(food);
        animal.groom();
        animal.pet();
        animal.exercise();
    } else if (animal.isThirsty()) {
        Bucket water = getWater();
        Animal.drink();
        animal.groom();
        animal.pet();
        animal.exercise();
        animal.train();
    } else {
        animal.groom();
        animal.pet();
        animal.exercise();
    }
}
```

After:

```
void feedAnimal(Animal animal) {
   if (animal.isHungry()) {
      Food food = obtainFood();
      food.prepare();
      animal.feed(food);
      careForAnimal(animal);
   } else if (animal.isThirsty()) {
      Bucket water = getWater();
      Animal.drink();
      careForAnimal(animal);
      animal.train();
   } else {
      careForAnimal(animal);
   }
}

void careForAnimal(Animal animal) {
      animal.groom();
      animal.pet();
      animal.exercise();
}
```

Example 2

This example shows a long and complex method that benefits from self-documenting.

Before:

```
boolean isInCheck() {
   boolean inCheck = false;
   Position kingsPosition =
               king.getPosition();
   for (Pawn pawn : pawns) {
      if (pawn.canAttack(kingsPosition)
         inCheck = true;
   }
   for (Rook rook : rooks) {
      if (rook.canAttack(kingsPosition)
         inCheck = true;
   }
   for (Knight knight : knights) {
      if (knight.canAttack(kingsPosition)
         inCheck = true;
   }
   for (Bishop bishop : bishops) {
      if (bishop.canAttack(kingsPosition)
         inCheck = true;
   }
   if (queen.canAttack(kingsPosition)
      inCheck = true;
   if (otherKing.canAttack(kingsPosition)
      inCheck = true;

   return inCheck;
}
```

After:

```
boolean isInCheck() {
  Position kingsPosition =
            king.getPosition();
  return pawnsCanAttack(kingsPosition) ||
    rooksCanAttack(kingsPosition) ||
    knightsCanAttack(kingsPosition) ||
    rooksCanAttack(kingsPosition) ||
    bishopsCanAttack(kingsPosition) ||
    queen.canAttack(kingsPosition) ||
    otherKing.CanAttack(kingsPosition);
}

boolean pawnsCanAttack(Position kingsPosition)
{
  return pieces.canAttack(pawns,
                kingsPosition);
}

boolean rooksCanAttack(Position kingsPosition)
{
  return pieces.canAttack(rooks,
                kingsPosition);
}

boolean knightsCanAttack(
                Position kingsPosition) {
  return pieces.canAttack(knights,
                kingsPosition);
}

boolean bishopsCanAttack(
                Position kingsPosition) {
  return pieces.canAttack(bishops,
                kingsPosition);
}

boolean piecesCanAttack(Piece[] pieces,
                Position kingsPosition) {
```

```
    boolean inCheck = false;
    for (Piece piece : pieces) {
        if (piece.canAttack(kingsPosition)
            inCheck = true;
    }
    return inCheck;
}
```

Example 3

This example shows how to extract a method from code that shares local variables with the code that is not extracted. If the extracted method only reads the variable's value, the variable can become a parameter for the extracted method. If the extracted method changes the value of the variable and the non-extracted code uses the changed variable, the extracted variable may need to be returned as the return value for the extracted method. If the method needs to return more than one value, consider extracting multiple methods instead of only one, or if the return values are cohesive, you may need to introduce a new class to hold the multiple values, which you may return. This example shows two read-only variables and one writable variable:

Before:

```
void shadeSkinnyRectangle(
              Rectangle rectangle){

   int height = rectangle.getHeight();
   int width = rectangle.getWidth();

   if (height * 2 > width) {
      int area = height * width;
      float scaledArea = (float) area *
                   SCALE_FACTOR;
      Color color;
      if (scaledArea <= SMALL_AREA)
         color = Color.RED;
      else if (scaledArea <= MEDIUM_AREA)
         color = Color.YELLOW;
      else
         color = Color.GREEN;

      rectangle.paint(color);
   }
}
```

After:

```
void shadeSkinnyRectangle(Rectangle rectangle)
{

   int height = rectangle.getHeight();
   int width = rectangle.getWidth();

   if (isSkinnyRectangle(height, width)) {
     Color color = determineColor(height,
                   width);
   rectangle.paint(color);
   }
}

boolean isSkinnyRectangle(int height,
                   int width) {
   return (height * 2 > width);
}

Color determineColor(int height, int width) {
   int area = height * width;
   float scaledArea = (float) area *
                   SCALE_FACTOR;
   Color color = null;
   if (scaledArea <= SMALL_AREA)
     color = Color.RED;
   else if (scaledArea <= MEDIUM_AREA)
     color = Color.YELLOW;
   else
     color = Color.GREEN;
   return color;
}
```

Pull Up Construct

Abstract

Subclasses have the same field or method. Move the construct into a superclass.

Discussion

As a result of refactoring, subclasses may end up with similar constructs such as fields or methods. If you can look through the code and determine that the fields or methods do the same thing, you can refactor them into a superclass [Normalization]. If the similar constructs exist in only a subset of the subclasses, you may be missing a superclass for the subset of subclasses. This missing superclass is a subclass of the original superclass.

Example

In this example, the Flintstone class and the Jetson class both have fields that represent birthdays. Although these fields have different names, the fields are logically equivalent. The refactored code moves the field into the Character super class.

Before:

```
class Character {
   ...
}

class Flintstone extends Character {

   Date dateOfBirth;
   ...
}

class Jetson extends Character {

   Date birthday;
   ...
}
```

After:

```
class Character {

   Date birthday;
   ...
}

class Flintstone extends Character {


   ...
}

class Jetson extends Character {


   ...
}
```

Replace Type Field with Inheritance

Abstract

A class has an immutable field that affects the behavior of the class. Remove the field and use inheritance to specialize the behavior.

Discussion

If you have a field in your class that you set at construction and never change, and several methods of the class check its value to behave differently, your class has an immutable field that affects the class' behavior. Replace the immutable field with polymorphism. A common indication that you have this situation is when one or more methods of the class have switch statements or cascading if-then-else's based on an immutable state value. Using polymorphism instead removes the switch statement [Normalization] and keeps all the related behaviors in the same class [Cohesion]. Note that sections of code that are common to all of the classes may be factored into the base class [Normalization].

Example

This is an example of a class representing vehicles. The constructor of the Vehicle class has a parameter that determines the type of vehicle. Different methods of the class check the vehicle type to figure out different characteristics about the vehicle.

Refactoring the Vehicle class allows each specific vehicle behavior type to have its own subclass with its own characteristics. Notice also that the use of polymorphism creates subclasses with true "is-a" relationships with the vehicle class.

Before:

```
class Vehicle {

   enum Type {
      TRUCK,
      SUV,
      MID_SIZE,
      COMPACT
   }

   Type type;

   Vehicle(Type type) {
      this.type = type;
   }

   double odometer = 0.0;
   double tankContents = 0.0;

   double getTankSize() {
      double tankSize = 0.0;
      switch(type) {
      case Type.TRUCK:
         tankSize = 40.0;
      break;
      case Type.SUV:
         tankSize = 30.0;
      break;
      case Type.MID_SIZE:
         tankSize = 25.0;
      break;
      case Type.COMPACT:
         tankSize = 12.0;
      break;
      }
      return tankSize;
   }

   double fillTank() {
```

```
      double tankSize = getTankSize();
      double amountNeeded = tankSize —
                      tankContents;
      tankContents = tankSize;
      return amountNeeded;
   }

   double tankPercentFull() {
      return 100 * tankContents /
                      getTankSize();
   }

   void Drive(double miles) {
      double milesPerGallon = 0.0;
      switch(type) {
      case Type.TRUCK:
         milesPerGallon = 15.0;
      break;
      case Type.SUV:
         milesPerGallon = 18.0;
      break;
      case Type.MID_SIZE:
         milesPerGallon = 22.0;
      break;
      case Type.COMPACT:
         milesPerGallon = 32.0;
      break;
      }

      tankContents -= miles / milePerGallon;
      odometer += miles;
   }
}
```

After:

```
class Vehicle {

   double odometer = 0.0;
   double tankContents = 0.0;

   abstract double getTankSize();

   double fillTank() {
      double tankSize = getTankSize();
      double amountNeeded = tankSize -
                    tankContents;
      tankContents = tankSize;
      return amountNeeded;
   }

   double tankPercentFull() {
      return 100 * tankContents /
                  getTankSize();
   }

   abstract double getMilesPerGallon();

   void Drive(double miles) {
      tankContents -= miles /
                  getMilePerGallon();
      odometer += miles;
   }
}

class Truck extends Vehicle {
   double getTankSize() {
      return 40.0;
   }

   double getMilesPerGallon() {
      return 15.0;
   }
}
```

```
class SUV extends Vehicle {
   double getTankSize() {
      return 30.0;
   }

   double getMilesPerGallon() {
      return 18.0;
   }
}

class MidSize extends Vehicle {
   double getTankSize() {
      return 25.0;
   }

   double getMilesPerGallon() {
      return 22.0;
   }
}

class Compact extends Vehicle {
   double getTankSize() {
      return 12.0;
   }

   double getMilesPerGallon() {
      return 32.0;
   }
}
```

Replace Type Field with Strategy

Abstract

A class has a field that changes from time to time and that affects the behavior of the class. Replace the field with a reference to a strategy object.

Discussion

If you have a field in your class that changes from time to time, and several methods of the class check its value to behave differently, your class has a type field that affects the class' behavior. You replace the field with a reference to a class that encapsulates the changing behavior. A common indication that you have this situation is one or more methods of the class have switch statements or cascading if-then-else's based on a field value. Using a reference to a strategy object instead removes the switch statement [Normalization] and keeps all the related behaviors in the same class [Cohesion]. Note that sections of code that are common to all of the classes may be factored into a strategy base class [Normalization].

Note that strategy should be used in these situations and not polymorphism. From a logical standpoint, strategies do not have an is-a relationship as is implied by inheritance. From a mechanics perspective, you cannot use inheritance because you cannot change the type of the object once it has been instantiated.

Example

Imagine building an artificially intelligent agent to play a board game. When the agent first starts playing the game, the agent uses a neutral strategy. If the agent is losing the game, then the agent may choose a strategy that is high-risk so as to be able to find a winning move. However, if the agent is winning, the agent chooses a more moderate strategy to try and maintain the lead.

This example shows such an agent. In the pre-refactored code, the agent keeps track of the mode, neutral, winning or losing. Then, based on the mode the agent makes moves. Refactoring maintains the three different strategies in separate anonymous classes. The agent maintains a reference to the appropriate strategy and changes the references as the state of the game changes.

The refactored code is a bit complicated due to the use of the enum and the anonymous inner classes. The reason for using the enum is the strategies are related constants (albeit code constants) – enums are a direct and computationally tractable way to represent related constants. However, the only way to create subclasses of the enum is with anonymous inner classes. Some programmers rightfully avoid anonymous inner classes because anonymous inner classes may only be tested indirectly. However, in this case the choice to use an enum requires the anonymous inner classes.

Before:

```
class Agent {

   enum GameMode {
      NEUTRAL,
      WINNING,
      LOSING
   }

   GameMode mode;

   Agent() {
      this.mode = GameMode.Neutral;
   }

   void setMode(GameMode mode) {
      this.mode = mode;
   }

   void makeMove() {
      switch(mode) {
      case GameMode.NEUTRAL:
         // Make a neutral move
      break;
      case GameMode.WINNING:
         // Make a conservative move
      break;
      case GameMode.LOSING:
         // Make a radical move
      break;
      }
   }
}
```

After:

```
interface GameModeMethod {
   void makeMove();
}
```

```
class Agent {

    enum GameMode implements GameModeMethod {
        NEUTRAL {
    void makeMove() {
       // Make neutral move
    }
        },
        WINNING {
    void makeMove() {
       // Make conservative move
    }
        },
        LOSING {
    void makeMove() {
       // Make radical move
    }
        };
        abstract void makeMove();
    }

    GameMode mode;

    Agent() {
        this.mode = GameMode.NEUTRAL;
    }

    void setMode(GameMode mode) {
        this.mode = mode;
    }


    void makeMove() {
        mode.makeMove();
    }
}
```

Chapter 11 - Orthodoxy-Based Rules

Today's software development is a team sport. Gone are the days of the lone guy locking himself in a basement and building an entire operating system. As such, developers need to work so as to facilitate and optimize the team effort.

Software development tools, such as programming languages, provide many different ways to do the same thing. Some of the things developers try to accomplish are innovative and require novel approaches. However, many of the things developers do have long-standing and established approaches. These customary approaches are what developers expect to see and when developers choose not to use customary approaches, these irregular approaches may hinder other team members as they wrestle with the implications of the approach.

Often, developers use non-standard approaches because they aren't familiar with the standard ways, or they want to be clever. It may be helpful to deviate from the standard if there is some concrete benefit, however, deviation for the sake of being clever has costs with no real benefits.

The rules in this chapter explain common deviations from standard development practices and how to fix them.

Acknowledge Exceptions

Abstract

A *catch* clause inadvertently ignores an exception. Have the *catch* clause perform some form of notification.

Discussion

Sometimes developers are forced to catch a checked exception but don't know what to do about it. In this case the worst thing to do is to silently catch the exception and continue on. Imagine trying to debug a program that is throwing an exception and there is no indication that program has thrown the exception. In the very least, print out the stack trace to an error log [Orthodoxy].

There are a few situations where code really does want to ignore an exception. In these cases it is appropriate to note in a comment in the *catch* clause that the exception is being purposely ignored. This comment lets readers of the code know that the code is not inadvertently ignoring the exception.

The philosophy for how to deal with exceptions is relatively recent in programming history. Originally the notions of type safety influenced language developers to include checked exceptions in languages. Checked exceptions are those exceptions that, when a method throws the exception, requires the method to include a throws clause in the signature of the method to tell callers of the method to expect the exception. While this sounds good in theory, the problem is that the caller of the method may not know how to deal with the exception, in which case the caller must modify its method signature to add the throws clause.

Now, imagine you have layered working software that requires a new method call at the lowest level to a method that throws a checked exception. Assuming the lowest caller does not know how to deal with the exception, all layers from the call on up must modify their method signatures.

Also consider that the checked exceptions are not the only exceptions that require attention. If a caller does not know how to deal with a checked exception, what is the difference between how the caller should respond to a checked exception that the caller does not know how to handle, and any other unchecked exception? In either case the caller will likely do the same thing, which is to propagate the exception to a higher level.

As a general rule, code should handle exceptions at the lowest level that understands how to handle the exception. However, since it is not always clear how to handle the exception at lower levels of code, the exception must be propagated to higher levels. Further, the higher the level of code, the less likely the code can do anything useful with the exception. This creates a dichotomy.

For truly fault tolerant systems, no exceptions may be ignored. Take, for example, a Mars rover. If the rover software were to throw an exception, it would be unacceptable to print out a stack trace and exit, but what else could the rover do? One option would be to log the error and try to reinitialize the system. Now if the system could handle unexpected exceptions in this way, the designer of the system might consider what other exceptions could also be handled in this manner. If there is no specific manner for dealing with a certain exception, the system might as well deal with it using the reinitialization strategy.

So fundamentally, there are two kinds of exceptions; those that the system can handle with a specific strategy and those that must be handled with a general strategy. Code should handle specific strategies at as low of levels in the software as possible. The code should handle all other exceptions at the highest level. Therefore, it makes little sense to have checked exceptions as they only clutter method signatures [Limit Interaction]. When code calls a method that throws a checked exception, if the calling code does not know how to deal with the exception and the system will handle the exception in the general case, it is probably best to wrap the exception with a non-checked exception in the catch clause and propagate the exception up to the general handler. The general handler should recognize the wrapped exceptions and unwrap them prior to logging the exception.

Example 1

This first example shows an exception that the code is inadvertently ignoring. The refactored code shows the minimal remedy – which is to print out a stack trace.

Before:

```
...
try {
    something...
}
catch (SomeException e) {
}
```

After:

```
...
try {
    something...
}
catch (SomeException e) {
    e.printStackTrace();
}
```

Example 2

It is important to remember that with this minimal remedy the program will continue to execute beyond the exception. If continued execution could have detrimental side effects, the code may need to wrap the exception and propagate the exception to a general handler. This example shows how to wrap an exception and handle it as a general exception.

Before:

```
class System {

   static void main(String[] args) {
      System system = new System();
      System.start();
   }

   void start() {
      ...
      method1();
      ...
   }

   void method1() {
      ...
      method2();
      ...
   }

   void method2() {
      ...
      File file = TheRootDirectory;
      try {
         // This reassignment is a bad idea,
         // but imagine code
         // that does this anyway
         file = findTheFileToDelete();
      }
      catch (SomeCheckedException e) {
         e.printStackTrace();
      }
      // Notice that if an exception occurs,
      // Executing beyond this point would be
      // disastrous
      file.delete();
      ...
   }
}
```

After:

```
class System {

   static void main(String[] args) {

   while (true) {
      try {
          System system = new System();
          System.start();
      }
      catch (Throwable e) {
         logException(e);
      }
     }
   }

   void start() {
      ...
      method1();
      ...
   }

   void method1() {
      ...
      method2();
      ...
   }

   void method2() {
      ...
      File file = TheRootDirectory;
      try {
         // This reassignment is a bad idea,
         // but imagine code
         // that does this anyway
         file = findTheFileToDelete();
      }
      catch (SomeCheckedException e) {
```

```
            MyUncheckedException exception =
               new MyUncheckedException(e);
            throw exception;
         }
         // Notice that if an exception occurs,
         // Executing beyond this point would NOT
         // be disastrous
         file.delete();
         …
      }
   }
}
```

Construct Well-formed Objects

Abstract

After constructing an object, the object requires the calling
code to use setter methods to put the object into a well-formed
state. Expand the constructor by adding the necessary
parameters.

Discussion

With the advent of dependency injection that uses XML to
construct objects, it has become fashionable to use
parameterless constructors and then use setters to put the
object into a well-formed state (please note that fashion is not
a design principle). While this may be necessary for
dependency injection, developers should avoid this approach
when possible. These incomplete constructors leave the
object only partially formed requiring setters to complete the
task. While it may be possible to construct the object using
setters, the constructors no longer explain all that is necessary
to construct the object [Direct Expression]. Further, if later
developers modify the object and add fields that must be
initialized in order for the object to be well formed, the
compiler will not be able to notify developers of the
inconsistencies [Orthodoxy, Normalization].

Example

Here is an example of a parameterless constructor for a Dog
class. After constructing the class, the calling code must set
various attributes for the dog. With this type of approach it is
difficult to know if and when the calling code has set all the
necessary attributes. This example shows the calling code
setting the name, color and weight attributes, but what about a
hasFleas attribute or a doesSlobber attribute? The refactored

code uses the constructor to identify the necessary attributes that put the object in a well-formed state.

Before:

```
Dog fido = new Dog();
fido.setName("Fido");
fido.setColor(Color.BROWN);
fido.setweight(45);
```

After:

```
Dog fido = new Dog("Fido", Color.BROWN, 45);
```

Limit Constructors to Construction

Abstract

A class' constructor constructs the class and performs some behavior. Separate the behavior into its own method.

Discussion

Some classes only have one behavior, so developers may be tempted to perform the behavior as part of the constructor. Instead, a constructor should place an object in a well-formed state – neither more nor less [Orthodoxy, Cohesion]. Adding behaviors to a constructor causes the constructor to do more than one thing, which means the constructor has temporal or procedural cohesion. Separating the behavior into its own method improves the cohesion for both the constructor and the method that encapsulates the behavior.

Example

This example shows a Game class. The only behavior this class has is to play, so the developer decided to lump the behavior in with the constructor. The refactored code separates the constructor from the play() method.

Before:

```
class Game {

   Game() {
      // set up the class
      // play the game
   }
}
```

After:

```
class Game {

    Game() {
        // set up the class
    }

    void play() {
        // play the game
    }
}
```

Remove Multiple Exits From Code Blocks

Abstract

A code block has multiple exits in the form of breaks, continues or returns. Modify the code to eliminate extra exits.

Discussion

Dijkstra defined structured programming as programs containing code blocks with only one entry point and only one exit point. Structured programming allows programmers to consider each code block in terms of its preconditions, invariants and post-conditions [Orthodoxy]. The common way of violating structured programming is the misuse of break, continue and return statements. These violations often indicate a poorly thought-out algorithm. Reflection on the algorithm will yield an understanding that can eliminate these extra exits.

This rule is highly violated today in the industry. However, with some reflection these violations may be eliminated with a more clear approach. After working through a few of these cases, it will become second nature as to how to maintain a structured approach. Structured approaches make the transition easier to develop for systems that require resource management; i.e., multi-threading, transactional systems and systems with unmanaged memory.

Note also that code may include a single break statement and still only have one exit (e.g., an infinite loop with a break). This type of loop is well structured. Therefore, it is not the break that makes the code unstructured, but it is the multiple exits from the code block (i.e., loop) that make the code unstructured.

Example

Here is an example of a method that searches through an array of strings for a particular string and returns the index of the target string. In the pre-refactored code example, the method returns in the middle of the loop if it finds the string or at the end of the loop if it does not find the string. The refactored code eliminates the return from the middle of the loop.

Before:

```
int findString(String[] strings, String
target) {

    for (int i=0; i < strings.length(); i++) {
        if (strings[i].equals(target))
            return i;
    }
    return -1;
}
```

After:

```
int findString(String[] strings,
                    String target) {

    int result = -1;
    for (int i = 0; (result == -1) &&
                (i < strings.length()); i++) {
        if (strings[i].equals(target))
            result = i;
    }
    return result;
}
```

Replace Exception with Test

Abstract

Code throws an exception on a condition the caller could have checked first. Change the caller to test first.

Discussion

Exceptions should be used only for unexpected behavior. Exceptions should not act as a substitute for conditional tests [Orthodoxy]. If code can reasonably expect the caller to check for the condition before calling the method, the code should provide a checking method to the caller and the caller should use it [Direct Expression].

One of the problems with using exceptions for expected behavior is that the exception may be misunderstood. In other words, the expected exception may actually occur for more than one reason. The handling code assumes the exception indicates the anticipated cause, but if the exception actually indicates a different problem, the problem will be very difficult to track down.

An additional problem with using exceptions for unexceptional conditions is that the code becomes a bit difficult to read. Since the norm is not to use exceptions for non-exceptional situations, the reader of the code must hesitate to digest the unorthodox use of the exception.

Example

This example has a method that maps a value for each period using an array. If the period is beyond any of the values in the array, the method returns zero. The pre-refactored code doesn't bother to check if the array index is in bounds, but instead tries to access the array value and handles the exception if the index is out of bounds. The refactored code does a simple test to make sure the index is within the bounds to avoid the exception.

Before:

```
double getValueForPeriod(int periodNumber) {
   try {
      return values[periodNumber];
   }
   catch (ArrayIndexOutOfBoundsException e) {
      return 0.0;
   }
}
```

After:

```
double getValueForPeriod(int periodNumber) {
   return (periodNumber < values.length)?
         values[periodNumber]:  0.0;
}
```

Use Exceptions for Exceptional Conditions

Abstract

Code uses exceptions for return values and return values for exceptions. Only use exceptions for exceptional conditions.

Discussion

Exceptions are a bit problematic because they break the definition of Structured Programming. It is not always immediately obvious what the effects of an exception may be. For example, methods that allocate resources should guard against exceptions by deallocating the resources in the event of an exception. Therefore, developers generally do not anticipate using exceptions as return values [Orthodoxy]. Using return values instead of exceptions clutters the code since the calling code must remember to check the return value and respond accordingly. Experience has shown that developers often overlook checking the return values. Not checking the return values in these situations causes errors to go undetected. When developers do check return values for errors, the code dealing with the return values obscures the flow of the calling code [Direct Expression]. Additionally, it may be necessary to duplicate code for recovering from return codes [Normalization] whereas developers can easily centralize the recovery code for exceptions without duplication.

Example

The following code segment shows code that must check return values to determine if an exception occurred. The result is complicated code with deep nesting. Using exceptions lets the code centralize the checking and resolve any errors in one location.

Before:

```
...
File file = open("xyz.txt");
if (file == null) {
   System.err.println("Error opening file");
} else {
   int n = file.read(byteArray);
   if (n == -1) {
      System.err.println("Error reading file");
      file.close();
   } else {
      ...
   }
}
```

After:

```
File file = null;
try {
   file = open("xyz.txt");
   file.read(byteArray);
}
catch (exception e) {
   e.printStack();
   if (file != null) file.close();
}
```

Chapter 12 - Conclusion

Recently I attempted to teach a class about these refactoring rules and their associated principles. I had class members review each of the rules and provide examples to illustrate the rules. Then I assigned students moderate software development projects. I expected them to employ the principles and rules in the software they developed.

One of the students came to my office to review the test cases he had developed for the software project. I reviewed the tests with him and also reviewed some of his code. I was disappointed to see that the code blatantly violated many of the refactoring rules that the students had attempted to learn.

As I poured through the code and found violations of the rules, I pointed them out to the student. After several of these, I had to reflect. This student was a reasonably bright student and appeared to be conscientious. So I had to wonder what the problem was. Why had he not observed the rules I had tried to teach him?

When I asked him why he did not observe the rules, he told me it was because there were just too many rules to remember. This response was, on the one hand a bit shocking to me, and on the other hand quite a reasonable answer. There are on the order of fifty rules. How could I expect a student to quickly remember all of them? Then I reflected on my own thinking. I found it strange that I could remember these rules quite easily and could quickly recognize violations. I am an older man with a tired brain and he was a bright young man. Why was I able to remember the rules so much easier than he?

As I pondered this question I realized that I really don't remember the rules; what I remember are the principles. The rules are merely manifestations of the principles. In fact, if one can understand the principles, it is no longer necessary to remember any of the rules because the violations will just stand out.

Perhaps as you read through the rules you had a special rule of your own. You may have examined each rule looking to see if the next rule is your favorite rule. You may have even reached the end of the book and not found your pet rule included in the list. You may think the author a scoundrel for not including this important rule. While you may be correct in that the author may indeed be a scoundrel, if you believe the author to be such, merely because of omitting your pet rule, then you have missed the point of the book.

The point of this book is *not* to teach rules for refactoring, but to outline important principles of software design. I have approached these principles from the perspective of refactoring rules because refactoring rules are concrete examples that illustrate the principles. Software developers easily relate to the rules, whereas trying to understand the principles becomes a difficult ethereal cognitive effort.

Although understanding the principles does require some mental exertion, it is important to do the reflection necessary to grasp the principles. The rules provide a gentle on-ramp, but you will need to reflect so as to cognitively cement the principles. Principles are important, because as we work from principles, we move out of the realm of mere opinion into an area with basis for our judgment.

Appendix A - The Software Design Pyramid

In 1943, Abraham Maslow introduced a hierarchy to describe human motivation. This hierarchy, now commonly known as Maslow's Hierarchy, describes motivations starting with basic physiological needs such as breathing/eating and moving to more esoteric needs like creativity. Maslow explained that the more basic needs must be fulfilled before a person can satisfy the esoteric needs. In other words, a person who is starving isn't concerned with being creative, but once a person is comfortable they will not starve, they may be inclined to think about creativity.

We may see software developers' concerns as having a similar hierarchy when creating software. These concerns include the following:
- Software function
- Software structure
- Software's subcomponent relationships
- Software abstraction
- Software future modification and extension
- Balancing risk

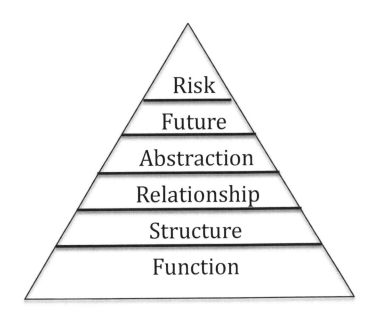

Software Development Hierarchy of Concerns

Software Function

The most fundamental and necessary concern for software is that the software does what it is supposed to – the software functions correctly. This is the primal concern for introductory programmers. They don't care about algorithmic elegance, object abstraction, the use of methods or even useful variable names. If the software does or doesn't do what it is supposed to, nothing else really matters.

It is no wonder novice programmers focus their attention so intently on function. Our thought processes are deceptively complex and describing, in a programming language, the actual process for accomplishing a task is a difficult endeavor. Novice programmers must experiment with translating thinking into programs until they become comfortable with basic notions of programming, like control flow and simple data types.

Software Structure

As programmers become comfortable that they can indeed convert conceptual processes into programs, they begin to become aware that there may be more than one way to represent these processes. Further, as developers become structurally aware, they realize that, although there are several ways to represent a process, some ways are better than others. The reasoning behind what makes one process representation (i.e., program) better than others make take many forms. One program might have fewer lines of code because the program has somehow eliminated redundancy. Another program may choose to employ a technique like recursion that seems to naturally represent the process.

As developers begin to become aware of software structure, their focus moves away from just making the program work towards making a program that works and is easy to understand. The structure of a program involves removing redundancy in both data and flow control, selecting clean algorithms and naming constructs to suggest their meaning. Structurally aware developers will spend time refactoring, extracting new methods to eliminate code they have copied and pasted. They may redesign algorithms to improve the program efficiency and they may also rename variables to help them remember what the variable represents.

Software Subcomponent Relationships

Armed with a realization that there are several ways to write a program and as a result of extracting methods to remove redundancy, developers begin to develop an intuition about the components that make up software. As these developers begin to build larger and more complex processes, they realize the need to organize software so that they can navigate its complexities.

In response to trying to find ways to organize the complexity of larger programs, developers stumble into the use of hierarchy as an organizing principle – the idea that larger constructs consist of smaller ones. The natural result of applying hierarchical approaches is that developers begin to clump related things in close proximity. Also, the use of the hierarchy helps developers naturally to limit the number of interacting parts. As developers begin to experience the reduced conceptual load that results from limiting interaction, they begin to seek to leverage this effect by constructing useful and purposeful barriers. These barriers limit scope and make it easier to conceptualize sub-processes.

Another design concept that often emerges at this stage of a developer's awareness is the notion of indirection. Developers realize, at some level, that indirection delays binding. For example, one might write a program to add two constants, say three and five. This program is only useful for adding these two specific numbers. In order to make the program more useful, it is necessary to delay the binding of the values the program adds until runtime. Programmers delay this binding by using variables instead of constants. This is indirection at work.

At the relationship awareness stage, developers may not have a full realization of the implications of indirection, but they begin to observe its affects in limited circumstances. This initial awareness is crucial in preparing the developer to move to the next level.

Software Abstraction

Given enough experience, developers begin to realize that there are naturally occurring ways to keep related things together. Their intuition leads them to identify clumps of related procedures and data that somehow *feel* right. These clumps are called *abstractions* and are the foundation of robust design.

As developers initially experience abstraction, they may find it difficult to articulate why some constructs fit together better than others. Introducing the concepts of coupling and cohesion may help developers strengthen their intuition. One way to explain this intuition is to view constructs that make up an abstraction as points in a mathematical graph of nodes and edges. In such a mathematical graph, abstractions form a tight-knit portion of the graph. This portion is tightly connected with edges between its constructs, but has few edges extending beyond the tight-knit section. When we feel the intuition of abstraction, our minds are identifying which constructs are tightly connected and which are not. This is fundamentally how we decide what we include in an abstraction.

The intuition of abstraction can be difficult to articulate, however, developers who have the intuition can easily recognize it in others. In this way, abstraction works as a secret handshake between developers. Developers of a development team usually can quickly identify those other members of the team who share this intuition. These developers will often band together and exclude those who do not have the abstraction intuition. It is as if they say to those without the intuition: it's an abstraction thing, you wouldn't understand.

Developers who have the intuition of abstraction can use it as a design power tool. Using abstraction developers can focus in on a detailed portion of a system until they understand it and then move to another. Developers can organize these abstractions using the concepts they have learned in more basic levels of design to form powerful systems where each abstraction is a simple and clean piece. Abstraction is the secret to being able to conceptualize complex systems.

Software Future Modification and Extension

As developers become proficient at identifying abstractions, they begin to see abstraction everywhere. These abstractions become very powerful in that they allow developers to identify and build abstractions that make the software much easier to adapt to future or unforeseen requirements. Developers who have developed well-abstracted software love to field requests to enhance the software because the abstractions in the software design seem to have anticipated the necessary changes. And those changes that have not been fully anticipated are usually easy enough to respond to with a couple of additional well-formed abstractions.

Developers who are anticipating the future needs and extension of software resonate to software design patterns. Design patterns emerge as abstractions of abstractions that are useful ways to organize software so that it handles the immediate needs, but also can be extended to future requirements. Those developers who have reached this level of awareness immediately understand the significance of a design pattern when they learn about it.

The study of design patterns also can benefit those who are striving to develop an awareness of future modification and extension. However, studying design patterns should not entail memorizing a name and a UML diagram. Instead, those studying design patterns should seek to understand why a design pattern is useful as well as the seeming subtle difference between patterns. An appreciation of the differences between patterns will drive home the point of the pattern and why it exists.

Balancing Risk

Developers who appreciate the beauty of abstraction and design patterns will be inclined to create lots of abstractions. After all, if a few abstractions are good, lots of abstractions must be better. This can lead to a problem in software development known as over-engineering. Over-engineering means that a developer builds structures that solve today's problems as well as tomorrow's problems, next year's problems and maybe even next century's problems. While there is nothing technically wrong with this, the development takes time and costs money. This time and money can sometimes outweigh the benefits of solving the immediate problems. The result is that no software gets built.

Very few developers truly reach this level. Some developers may claim to be at this level, but more often they are inept in software design and are trying to use this as an excuse to cover their ineptitude.

Usually over-engineering occurs in software development when a very strong designer looks down the road and anticipates a problem. The problem may be a very practical problem, but perhaps a bit unlikely. Still the developer convinces the design team that, even though the problem is a bit unlikely, the right thing to do is to solve the problem. Usually the problem is not too difficult to resolve anyway. However, once the design team accepts this problem as a reality that must be fixed, the solution may lead to another problem that should also be fixed. The design team seems to forget that the original problem is unlikely and therefore this subordinate problem is more unlikely. Instead, the design team tackles the subordinate problem as well. The subordinate problem(s) may also lead to further extensions. Eventually the team becomes so high centered that they can't complete the software for today's needs.

Developers who have experienced over-engineering and have an appreciation of balancing the risk of over-engineering with the payoff of making the software functionally complete for today's problems have reached a level of awareness of risk balancing. Notice that achieving this level of awareness requires significant experience. Developers must first climb the levels of the design hierarchy one by one until they become experts at abstraction and anticipating future needs. Then these developers must be involved in at least a couple of over-engineered projects so that they appreciate the costs of over-engineering. Only then is the developer able to accurately assess and balance risk.

For those who achieve the level of balancing risk, it is a precarious position. Like any balancing act, they must maintain vigilance that they are indeed maintaining balance and not leaning too much to one side or the other. One way to try and maintain the balance is to consciously identify problems and solutions without committing to their realization – sort of like keeping the answer in your hip pocket in the advent of the problem becoming a real threat. Then observe how events transpire. Should things unfold in such a way that the problem becomes real, the experienced developer will recognize the increased risk and move to introduce the solution. In the meantime, the developer does not expend effort to create the solution, but does make sure the software does not preclude the introduction of the solution if and when necessary.

Principle Index